SITES · SCENES · STORIES

Italy under my

skin

My travels the past 30 years

By Joe Reina
Author of The Goat Sleeps In The Kitchen

ISBN 978-1-68526-686-8 (Paperback)
ISBN 979-8-88644-533-6 (Hardcover)
ISBN 978-1-68526-687-5 (Digital)

Covenant Books
11661 Hwy 707
Murrells Inlet, SC 29576
www.covenantbooks.com

To David Phillips.
Joe Mocca.

FOREWORD

I'm Sicilian by marriage. My loving wife, Mary Rose, née Angeleri, and I had a very good friend, Nick Maniscalco, a kind and generous man. Like me, Nick was a Chicago lawyer. Unlike me, Nick did it all. Personal injury, criminal law, immigration, real estate, you name it. On the infrequent occasion that Nick lacked the requisite legal expertise himself; he had a guy who did. So when Nick's cousin needed a trademark lawyer for his shoe company, I was Nick's guy. That is how I met Joe Reina more than thirty years ago. Since then, Joe and his wife, Laurie, have had a few projects for me and introduced me to other attorneys and clients, and most importantly, we have become good friends. Like Joe and Laurie, Mary Rose and I have traveled throughout Italy and share a passion for the country and its people.

Italy Under My Skin is about Joe Reina's success in the shoe business, the beautiful people who Joe and Laurie met along the way that became lifelong friends, and his boundless love for Italy. Italy is a country like no other—incomparable history, art, architecture, natural beauty, cuisine, and wine. These are all excellent reasons to visit, but there is much more to Italy. The culture, lifestyle, and the warmth of the Italian people are what makes it unique. Joe's stories from his extensive travel throughout Italy and Sicily bring those experiences to life. In Portofino, for example, Joe relates a story of a tiny *osteria*, ten tables inside and six outside. Grandma was in the kitchen, and Grandpa was sitting at the bar with a glass of *vino*, watching over the help, most of whom were family members. The smells emanating from the kitchen sent Joe back to his childhood on The Hill in St. Louis, waking up Sunday mornings to the aromas from his mom's kitchen. The food was great, the house wine was better, and the bill was almost nothing. Experiences like this can be found in nearly every city, town, and village.

Joe captures the warmth of the Italian people. He writes of the generosity of an Italian shoe factory owner who embraced Joe and Laurie and welcomed them into his family. They overcame a language barrier to build a lasting relationship based on mutual trust and respect. He also writes of the warmth of relative strangers. In Milan, Joe and Laurie were denied admission to see *The Last Supper* by Leonardo DaVinci because of a ticketing error. Sitting outside, Laurie complemented a young museum guide on his sneakers. A conversation ensued, and it turned out that young man was from the same town in Sicily as the Reina family. He found a spot for Joe and Laurie on the next tour. It pays to make conversation.

In *Italy, Under My Skin*, Joe Reina provides insights that escape the usual guidebooks. Joe kept a detailed book of his four decades of travel throughout Italy and Sicily. Whenever he discovered a great hotel or a fantastic restaurant, it went into the book. Joe has provided travel recommendations to friends and family members over the years. Now, at the urging of those friends and family, he decided to share his experiences with the world. Regarding hotels, for example, Joe and Laurie discovered a small boutique hotel in a great location near the Spanish Steps in Rome. The rooms were beautiful and at half the price of better-known guidebook hotels. *Italy Under My Skin* includes descriptions of Joe's favorite restaurants in Rome, Milan, Florence, Verona, Assisi, and many other cities. Joe loves good wine. He researched Italian wineries and shares his favorites. He also wisely advises that you cannot go wrong with a carafe of the local wine. Italian restaurants take great pride in quality. They know the regional vineyards that produce excellent quality but might lack the distribution of the big guys. Not surprisingly, these local wines pair amazingly well with regional cuisine. Joe's best advice of all is don't delay your trip to Italy. He laments that his first trip to Italy was when he was forty-four. For me, it was forty-five. Why didn't we go sooner?

By the same token, why delay your next trip? *Italy Under My Skin* has renewed my itch to start planning our next trip to Italy.

The shoe business brought Joe Reina to Italy. For me, it was my wife's heritage and our thirst for travel. Our experiences have been different but parallel. Mary Rose and I can relate to the tiny *osteria* with simple, fantastic food and wine. In addition, we have our own discoveries, like finding beautiful hand-painted ceramics in Ravello. For the reader, whether it is your first trip to Italy or twenty-first, there are unique discoveries of your own waiting for you. *Italy Under My Skin* can help you find them.

Paul Juettner, Esq.

ACKNOWLEDGMENTS

I will be eternally grateful to my cousin, Dr. Hugh Ingrasci, for his contribution. To Dave Phillips, one of the world's great retired photographers, for the photos of our trip together with his lovely wife in Italy in 2006.

Thanks to Phyllis Fresta for her photos of our trip with my buddy Joe in 2000.

My sincere gratitude to Patricia Benesh of AuthorAssist.com for guiding me through the manuscript from day one.

And I would be remiss, if not to mention, Michelle Holmes and the staff at Covenant Books for all their help.

My sincere gratitude to Carolyn Langston for proofreading the story. She is making me a better writer.

PROLOGUE

In 1980 at age forty-four, I decided to go to Italy for the first time with my friend Cliff Abbey, who had been there numerous times. We flew to Stuttgart, and I picked up my first Mercedes. The combined joy of the car and visiting my homeland kept me in excited anticipation for weeks before the departure date.

We had lunch at the factory when we arrived while they made final checks on the car, and finally the director came to get us and handed me the keys, a joyous moment I will never forget.

A kid from The Hill in St. Louis was picking up an automobile in Germany, which was not even in my wildest dreams growing up in south St. Louis.

Driving through Italy was part two of the dream. And that car remains in the family, passed on to my son, Michael, in 2002.

Cliff and I drove to Zurich the first day, spent the night, and departed the next day for Portofino. I loved walking around the town. Our lunch was in a small *osteria*, a tiny place with only ten tables inside and six outside. The smells emanating from the kitchen sent me back to my childhood, waking up Sunday mornings to the aromas from my mom's kitchen. Cliff said, "These types of ristoranti were typical all through Italy. The grandma was usually in the kitchen, the grandpa sat at the small bar with a glass of vino, and watched over the help; most of the help were family members. We chose to eat outside. The weather was incredible, the sun was glistening on the water, and I continued to wonder if I was really in Italy. I learned another thing. Cliff ordered a carafe of house red to go with our pasta and meatballs, and it was as good, as any red I had ever tasted. The best was yet to come—panna cotta for dessert! The surprise was the *conta* (the bill), just under twenty dollars, and Cliff advised no tipping in Italy. He said, "Sometimes if you are in an upscale restaurant and you have an unusual dinner, maybe tip ten percent."

After lunch, Cliff suggested we walk to the famed Splendido Hotel. I was impressed and took a brochure. However, I was shocked when I converted the rates from lire to dollars. It was six hundred dollars a night.

We spent two nights there, and next, he drove to Florence (hereafter Firenze).

We stopped at a coffee shop. Cliff pulled out a notebook scribbled with a list of hotels and restaurants. After we finished our cappuccino and pastry, we started making our rounds, searching for a hotel.

August is the height of the vacation period for Italians themselves. First lesson: never travel to Italy without reservations, especially in August. After finding no vacancy in the city center, we ended up at the Hotel Villa Della Cora, a magnificent, expensive hotel on the outskirts of Firenze.

We unpacked and went down to the bar for an aperitif, discussed dinner, and ended up at the concierge desk. Once again, Cliff referred to his notebook and suggested several restaurants. Every one of his suggestions was futile. They were booked. Next lesson: the concierge usually gets a cut from the restaurant for recommendations. We ended up in a typical tourist restaurant with mediocre food. Never did I return to that restaurant in all my trips to that beautiful city.

After dinner, we strolled to the city center, which began my never-ending love for one of the most beautiful, romantic cities in the world. I could not believe the art on the streets. There were more statutes, monuments, and frescos in plain view than in most museums. And for the next two days, we enjoyed incredible weather. Sunshine drenched us. I had trouble believing I was strolling the streets of Firenze. There is no way to describe the city unless you have a camera and an artistic mind. There are more interesting historic buildings, more interesting people, and beautiful piazzas than in any city I have ever visited. Our two days there with no specific agenda was a mistake. I vowed to study the city for my return.

I was not feeling well the morning we departed and asked Cliff to drive to Rome, our next destination. I slept most of the way, and when we arrived at our hotel, the Excelsior on the Via Veneto, we had to call for a doctor. He didn't speak English. He determined I needed rest because I had no fever; with hand signals, he advised me to sleep. I decided to learn some Italian, and that the old Sicilian dialect my parents spoke was not effective.

Cliff stayed until the next day and departed for Amsterdam. My girlfriend, Cathy Berlinger, was due to arrive for the remainder of the trip.

On Saturday, I took a taxi to the airport to pick her up and got the next lesson. I was unaware there were two airports in Rome. Once again, my lack of basic Italian surfaced. After an hour of sitting, the driver got out of the cab and went inside to check on the flight to see what the delay was and learned that the flight had already arrived at the other airport. It was an hour to the other side of Rome. Two hundred dollars in taxi fees later, we finally picked up Cathy. Be reminded there were no cell phones in 1980.

We spent the weekend in Rome. She had been there, and she knew the city and showed me the sights. We had delightful dinners, and I got a taste of the eternal city. She took me to see the main attractions, the Colosseum, the Trevi Fountain, the Pantheon, and Piazza Navona. However, what was missing was the background, the history, the story behind them.

On Monday, we departed with the Mercedes for Positano. Next lesson: exiting Rome was a nightmare, especially considering neither of us spoke Italian, but finally, we were on the autostrada, heading for Naples and the Amalfi Coast. The drive along the sea was a delight.

We arrived in Positano early afternoon and checked into the famed Le Sirenuse Hotel, thanks to Cathy, who was more organized than Cliff. She also had the hotel make dinner reservations that night at a fine restaurant in town. Our time there was beyond my wildest expectations. No crowds and perfect weather. At that time, it was a beautiful, inexpensive town.

It was a sleepy little village, almost unheard of. Most people that traveled to the Amalfi coast went to Sorrento and Capri.

We had some delightful dinners and some that were mediocre because we depended on the concierge for suggestions and reservations. And I made a mental note to read about the best restaurants next time I return.

We departed and drove back to Rome, where I parked the car in a previously determined garage and filled out the paperwork to ship it to Chicago. The next day, we flew to Paris. Once again, Cathy was well-organized, and through her family travel agent, we had a very nice hotel and dinner reservations the first night.

We returned to Chicago after three nights in Paris. I enjoyed Paris, once again because Cathy knew her way around, but it did not compare to Italy. For weeks afterward, I shared Italy with friends and family, vowing to get back as soon as possible. I became obsessed with returning. My Sicilian blood would erupt while stuck in traffic or in an idle moment, like a dormant volcano. I could not get the trip out of my mind.

In 1984, I went into the sandal business with a partner importing a great product from Assisi, Italy. This ushered in the love, desire, and need to return. The sandal had, previously, never been imported into the United States. We actually launched a new footwear category with every major department and shoe store. It brought on the trips that have spanned thirty years.

This is my tale of love, romance, history, food, wine, and experiences in Italy, initially conducting business and later pure pleasure. I began recording hotels, sites, restaurants, historical events, things to do and see. What to avoid, how to maximize time, how to best spend money. And over the years, I have read several books about Italy and Sicily, allowing me to advise what to do and see and where to stay and eat.

When called upon by friends and family members, and associates, I have some authority about those subjects. I taught myself enough Italian to get by with no problems. Not fluent, but enough to understand and conduct both business and pleasure and enjoy our trips more.

This book is designed to help the reader prepare for all eventualities. Throughout the story, I write about the sites, cities, and small towns—their history, hotels, restaurants, things that are personal—which may not appear in other books or on the internet. You will want to note them as you read.

In general, be organized. Read about the places you plan to visit. Avoid the tourist restaurants and typical tourist traps. Study the history and culture. Use the train system. It is essential to understand the culture and appreciate the quality of life. If affordable, hire a guide in the major cities.

For the reader who has been there and have seen the sites mentioned, my historical knowledge will help to enjoy those experiences again. The reader touring for the first time will be better prepared for questions such as what to pack, what to expect concerning possible delays, and what to know about the geographical layout of the country.

For all travelers, it is important to understand the quality of Italian life. People and families take preference over all else. Italians live life first. Everything else comes last.

CHAPTER 1

Italy's Contributions to the World

I t is impossible to imagine the world without pasta, pizza, prosciutto, parmigiano, lasagna, risotto, melanzana (eggplant), espresso, cappuccino, great reds, and supreme white wines. Italy exports more wine than any other country in the world and some of the best olive oil.

And what about Verdi, Puccini, Donizetti, Caruso, Mario Lanza, Pavarotti, Sinatra, and Tony Bennett.

Let's give credit to Italy for the artistry of Michelangelo, Leonardo DaVinci, Raphael, Botticelli, Caravaggio, Titan, Donatello, Giotto, Bernini, Bellini, Tintoretto, Brunelleschi, and Modigliani.

Rome September 1990

My third trip to Rome was for both pleasure and business. This time, I was with my girlfriend, Laurie Granato. We had started dating seriously that summer and were working on the renovation of two large industrial buildings I was part owner of. Laurie is an architect, and her boss was a partner in the two projects.

This was Laurie's first trip to Italy. I had been back in 1985 with my daughter, Kelly. I learned to keep notes on the previous trip, and we had reservations for everything, hotels, restaurants, and sites.

We spent two nights in Rome, and for the first time with Laurie, we took what has become a traditional walk from the fountain of Trevi, down to the Pantheon, with a stop for a slice of pizza just south of the Piazza del Pantheon. Then on to the Piazza Navona.

Let's stop here. There are hundreds of books on Rome's sites. They all suggest these incredible three jewels! The Fountain is magical. The movie *Three Coins in the Fountain* created an unbelievable event for people to turn their back to it and throw three coins over their shoulder. In doing so, the myth is said to guarantee one will be sure to return. Laurie and I had to partake in the tradition.

The fountain is located in the Trevi district of Rome, hence the name. It was initially designed and constructed by an architect named Nicola Salvi, but he died during construction, and it was completed by Giuseppe Pannini. The water from the Fountain came from an aqueduct that supplied Rome with water for the baths. That aqueduct dates back to 20 BC and is located over ten miles away!

Originally, Bernini was commissioned to redesign an existing fountain, but it was never executed.

Later, the current Pope commissioned Salvi to build it.

Continuing our walk to the Pantheon, Laurie and I marveled at the structure of the building that was originally built by Emperor Agrippa. But it burned and was later rebuilt by Hadrian and completed around 126 AD.

Laurie, being an architect, was amazed at the size of this incredibly designed building and questioned the perfect circle opening in the ceiling. We learned the reason: it was to bring light into it.

We listened through phones about a brief history and discovered the great Roman artist Raphael is buried there. Also that the columns were brought in from Egypt. We were both astounded at how impossible it was to believe. It was 1800 years ago. How did they transport the columns? I said, "It is amazing to me that Rome has allowed this building to remain intact for all these years. In the States in a location like this, there would be condos on this site!"

Next we stopped just south of the Piazza for Italy's idea of fast food: pizza. This pizzeria had room for four people to stand, no tables.

A glass-enclosed counter displayed various pizzas baked in large rectangular pans. The smell spilled out onto the narrow street, no way to resist it. I swear they have a fan circulating that draws people to the place. The pizza options were sausage, zucchini, prosciutto, melanzana, buffalo mozzarella, and margarita. A lovely lady pointed to our choice, showed an approximate cut, and weighed it. The screen in front of the scale showed the price. She then put the pizza in a small oven to heat and brought it out. It was folded like a sandwich into a paper napkin that was two-sided, wax on one side where the pizza rested and the other side to be used after we ate to wipe our mouths and hands. Ah, the artistry of the Italians. We found one slice did not do the trick, and we both had seconds. We never take that walk and bypass that place. Also, right next door was a gelato shop. We had that on the return from our next stop.

We proceeded on the short walk to the Piazza Navona. A piazza is a square, or rectangular plaza, almost always with a beautiful church or a very important building. Many have historical significance.

In my opinion, without question, this is one of the top three piazzas in all of Italy. It was originally a sports facility in the first century. There are three beautiful fountains: the Fountain of Moor by Giacomo della Porta, the Fountain of Neptune, and the most famous, the Fountain of Four Rivers, by Gian Lorenzo Bernini. About the time the Pope commissioned Bernini to create the fountain in the sixteenth century, he commissioned Architect Borromini (Bernini's archrival) to design and build the church Saint Angeles in Agone across a narrow street from Bernini's fountain.

When Bernini learned of this, he became incensed. His largest statue is situated on his side, facing the church with his hand outstretched, pointing directly at the church. Bernini told Borromini, "My stature will be here when your church falls, and he will catch it!"

The piazza is surrounded by outdoor cafes and restaurants designed for the apparent throngs of tourists. Unless you are starving, please consider restaurants in Rome suggested later in this chapter for lunch and dinner.

We spent the next two days at the Colosseum and the Vatican, wasting a great deal of time standing in lines and learned a vital lesson. If you can afford it, hire a guide. You bypass the long lines and go right in. In one day, it is possible to see the Colosseum, walk old Rome (Forum) and stop for a nice one-hour lunch, reunite with the guide and tour the Vatican and St. Peter's, and be back at your hotel in time for a late afternoon cocktail.

Positano

On the third day, we departed Rome by train to Naples. I had secured a driver to pick us up at the station and drive us to Positano. It was a delightfully sunny day for one of the most scenic drives along any sea in all of Italy. The sun glistened across the beautiful Tyrrhenian Sea, and once again, we both felt how good it was to be alive, with warm feelings about that great country.

Laurie said, "Joe, I have no idea how I can ever repay you for this. So far, this is way beyond everything I have heard and read about this country. I was so excited when we discussed the trip initially, having read a few books back in my college days and the movies about it, but nothing compares with being here with you."

I said, "Laurie, I am enjoying it too, especially with you here." She had no idea as to some of the surprises ahead."

We arrived about lunchtime and checked into Le Sirenuse Hotel, and when the bellman opened the drapes, both of us were wowed by the ocean view. We did not unpack and strolled down to the walk along the beach and had pizza at Chez Black. The owner, a lady, embraced us as if we were locals. So typical of the Italian warmth, no attitude of any kind.

Laurie asked, "Can we walk around and see the town? I would like to buy something for my mom and grandmother." Shopping this unique village, she purchased two very nice gifts, and later we stumbled into a small art gallery, featuring paintings by a single artist named Diviccio.

Laurie showed me a beautiful knife palette painting depicting the town from the beach.

"Laurie, I have to have this." And I bought the piece.

After some rest and sun, we had a glass of wine out by the dining room. Later by taxi, we went up the top of the hill to the beautiful San Pietro Hotel for dinner. Laurie said, "Joe, this is, without a doubt, the most beautiful place in the world." I agreed. "Laurie, it is one of my favorite places. It was booked solid, or we would be staying here. I am delighted to be sharing it with you. This is a long way from the hectic schedule we have been dealing with on those two vacant buildings we are developing."

We had a great dinner and took a walk back in town afterward and a nightcap at the hotel before retiring.

At breakfast the following day, I suggested we take the local bus to Ravello.

Laurie said, "This is your deal. I am willing to do whatever you choose. Let's go."

We took the bus to Amalfi, changed buses, and took the winding road to this tiny village with an incredible view of the coast and sea. There are no words to describe some places. Ravello is one of them. While you can walk the town in an hour, you can't observe all the splendid views in that hour. It is so picturesque. Whenever I suggest the Amalfi Coast and Positano for my friends to see Ravello, I always advise them to take a day to go there for lunch and spend time enjoying this hidden gem tucked into the corner of the mountain. It is one of Italy's well-kept hideaways.

Gore Vidal chose to spend the latter years of his life there. Our trip was short-lived, but we both vowed on the next trip to spend a few more days in this quaint, little village, where it seemed time sat still for 500 years! Laurie asked to have lunch there, and we did. "Be sure to dine at Salvatore Ravello."

I felt the pressure of the two Chicago building developments we were involved in lifted from my shoulders, as well as the business problem and main reason for this trip.

On Friday, our driver picked us up for the return to the Naples train station for our return to Rome.

We were due to meet up with my Chicago attorney, Arnold Silvestri, for a meeting on Monday in Assisi.

In 1984, along with a partner, I began importing a sandal from Italy and literally launched a new category in the footwear industry. The brand name was Sensi. The sandal was made of polyvinyl chloride and was unique. It was both fashionable and functional. The footbed was perforated, which allowed sand or water to flow through and out the side of the sole that was also perforated.

We sold it to every department store and every major shoe store in the United States, and it was a huge success at retail. By 1989, we had ventured into all kinds of beach-related products.

My partner and his wife were in charge of product development and for five years expanded the brand into gifts and accessories unrelated to the sandal. The sandal soon became a stepchild to all the other items.

That year we also launched a sneaker called Superga, the number one selling shoe in Italy. Again, the sandal took a back seat to it!

I was not in favor of all this diversity. My partner, his wife, and I had a falling out, and we decided to split. They took distribution rights of all the gift items and accessories. The sandal and Superga distribution rights came to me. But there was a hitch. I inherited a $1,100,000 debt at the bank. My name was on the hook with a personal guarantee.

Before the split, my partner tried to buy my interest and that of a silent partner. At that time, I had decided it was best for me to step aside while he attempted to seek financing and also to set up a warehouse in Miami, where he lived. We both agreed that it should only take a few months. It was April, and we set a closing date for August 31, 1990. But he failed to get a loan. In August, we met in Chicago and reached an agreement with him taking the gifts and accessories sitting in the warehouse.

We signed the agreement and went our separate ways. So Laurie and I were on our way to Assisi to pick up the pieces.

We met in Rome over the weekend with the attorney, and on Monday, we departed for Assisi, for the meeting with the Sensi factory people. Arnold had gone to school in Perugia, the sister city for Assisi, and was fluent in the dialect of the area. This was needed because Mr. Sensi did not speak English. I had started picking up a few Italian words, some of which helped bring back my two years of high school Italian, but I needed a fluent translator for this business meeting.

The main reason for the meeting was to finalize moving the license from my former partner's name to my company name. He, the former partner, had conveniently used his name personally for the license. Having met Mr. Sensi only once briefly, I was concerned about getting official control of the distribution rights to the sandal.

We sat at the table with the Sensi attorney, along with Mr. Sensi's son and daughter, who worked in the business. Before we could get into the license agreement, Lorenzo Sensi asked, "Did you bring me a check?" I asked, "For what? Our records show we do not owe you anything."

He replied, "That is not true. You owe us $104,000 that was due to be paid in June. And there are 40,000 pairs of sandals sitting in my warehouse that your former partner ordered to be shipped last February. He kept postponing delivery. That's another $50,000 you owe us!"

I asked to use the phone, called my office, told my bookkeeper to call in my former accountants and have them immediately audit the books. I asked her to search the computer through the year and track every account payable for Sensi and call me back after the review.

We tabled all this and began the negotiation of the license. By lunchtime, we finished that, settling on a five-year agreement. Mr. Sensi (Lorenzo) complimented me for never being late on any payment heretofore and could not understand why we were late. I explained I had stepped out during the transition, hence the delay.

After lunch, I received a call from my bookkeeper I was dreading. My former partner had taken on a CFO to secure his line of credit. He zeroed out all accounts payable on our books. Not only did we owe $104,000, but we had an additional $60,000 in bills due!

I promised Lorenzo as soon as I returned to Chicago, I would send a check. As to the 40,000 pairs sitting in his warehouse, I explained that there was a problem. They were last year's colors and styles, and it was the end of the season. I needed time to dispose of them, but I accepted the responsibility. Even though I never ordered them, he agreed. (Upon my return, I learned there were an additional 40,000 pairs of the same colors sitting in my warehouse!)

One might ask, why did you take the license in the first place? There was a simple answer to that question: it was the $1.1M loan at American National Bank and my personal guarantee.

There was nothing I could do to my former partner. We had signed a hold harmless agreement in the contract. That was hard for me to understand. I had known him for sixteen years. I could not believe he did this to me. It dominated my mind for the next two days.

I had trouble sleeping. My mind kept circling back to when he first arrived on the scene in Chicago, working with me as a young twenty-two-year-old rookie salesman for the Arrow Company. I took him under my wing and treated him like a son, giving him every opportunity to make a name for himself. We had become good friends, even after he left the company and moved to California.

When he found the Sensi Sandal, he called me, and I told him to get on a plane and go see Mr. Sensi and secure the license.

He did not put any money into the business. I had all we needed to get started, and I structured the deal initially fifty-fifty. I refused to take advantage of him regarding the financial imbalance. We always drew the same salary. Not once did I challenge anything he did.

I had to set aside my utter disbelief and concentrate on the rest of the trip. I was determined to enjoy Assisi with Laurie.

We stayed at the Savoy Hotel for two days and had dinner at La Pallota, a small family-owned restaurant. The husband greeted guests while the Nonna cooked in the kitchen with the mom and the son and daughter serving. Because Arnold could speak the language, we were treated royally. Arnold told our server we were under the weather, and in a matter of minutes, she brought us a bowl of hot *zuppa di brodo con pastina*, chicken broth with small baby pasta. I immediately thought of my mom. How many times I came home from school feeling exactly the same way? I could never forget her putting the same bowl of soup in front of me and making me go to bed.

I recorded another lesson in my head after absorbing Arnold's mastery of the Italian language. "I have to learn to speak this language, especially now that I am doing business with Sensi."

Firenze

On Wednesday, Laurie and I departed for Firenze by train. Laurie turned to me and said, "I can't believe how calm you stayed when you realized what your former partner did to you."

I said, "It is worse than the financial part. After I stepped out, he changed the sales force to an all-encompassing group that specialized in selling gifts and accessories, and sales for the sandal dropped substantially. As to staying calm, my Sicilian temper is boiling." She asked, "What are you going to do?"

"I have to start all over again."

"But, Joe, you have this major responsibility with the administration and financial position of the two buildings with your partners back in Bellwood and Broadview. How are you going to handle everything?"

"One day at a time, Laurie. Right now, we are heading to one of my favorite cities in the world, and I will tackle these problems when we return. Nothing I can do about it now. I plan to hire people to do what needs to be done, and you are in that picture."

We took a taxi to our hotel Loggiato dei Serviti, a restored fifteenth-century monastery belonging to the same family for four hundred years with only nineteen rooms. It is in a great location and walking distance to everything. Another lesson: Don't even think of trying to drive in Firenze. Only taxis are allowed to drive in the city center of that remarkable city.

We unpacked and walked to the duomo cathedral, without question, one of the top three churches in all of Italy. After walking around the church, Laurie asked, "Are we going to walk up the stairs to the top?" I said, "You do that. I will meet you outside on the steps. There is no better place I know to watch people." The weather was perfect, a great time to travel Italy.

Later we walked across the street to the baptistery, and I explained the history to Laurie. The enormous bronze doors dated back to the twelfth century, and these were replicas. The originals are safely stored in a museum in the city.

They are called the Gates of Paradise and were created in the fifteenth century by a goldsmith named Lorenzo Ghiberti. They weigh approximately three tons and are seventeen feet tall. Michelangelo called the three doors faith, hope, and charity, humility, fortitude, temperance, and justice.

We then strolled up the street, and I took her to the Cantinetta dei Verrazzano for focaccia, made in the typical open-hearth wood-fired *forno* (oven). Displayed in sizeable rectangular cooking pans, it was prepared with various vegetables and cheeses and prosciutto. Only in Italy. We made our selections, and the lady took them and put them in the *forno* to warm. We took two glasses of red and sat at a communal table with people speaking many different languages, and on the way out, because it is also a bakery, we shared a fresh fig tart.

We spent the rest of the afternoon exploring the city with no agenda. We walked to the Piazza della Signoria and later returned there for a coffee, sitting outside on what was perhaps the nicest day, weather-wise, of the trip.

Laurie smiled and said, "I am almost afraid to ask what you have planned for dinner tonight, Mr. Reina."

"I thought I once asked you to call me, Joe." We both laughed.

"Tonight, Ms. Granato, we are dining at one of the top ten restaurants in Firenze. Without question, they have the best wine cellar in this town."

"Joe, now that we have gotten to know each other, you may call me Laurie."

It was agreed to meet in the hotel bar for a drink and later to walk to Enoteca Pinchiorri for dinner. Walking into the restaurant, we were greeted by the maitre'd, who said, "*Buonasera, signora*. Welcome back, *signore* Reina. We have your favorite table ready for you."

I ordered a bottle of Cabreo, our favorite white wine, mainly because I was unable to read the enormous wine list. Another lesson: learn Italian wines. I toasted Laurie, "Here's to you, kid."

"Oh, so now you're Humphrey Bogart? Do I look like Ingrid Bergman? I thought we were in Italy. That scene from *Casablanca* took place in Paris, Mr. Reina. Please, can we get back to Italy?" We both laughed.

After sampling the wine and hors d'oeuvres, I said, "Laurie, as you know, I have been a bachelor for the past nineteen years, would you consider changing that situation?"

Laurie, laughing, said, "That has to be the all-time great proposal. The answer is yes. When do you want to do this?"

"Let's do it next spring," I said. "First, let's meet each other's families." We set the date for April 7, 1991.

"How long have you been planning this?"

"I wanted to get involved with you ever since we first went to the Merchandise Mart in Chicago in 1985 to buy furniture for my mom, but I feared because of the twenty-year age difference, you'd refuse to be involved. But then when we started working on the buildings and seeing each other, I began thinking of bringing you here to this very city and to this restaurant to make my move!"

"Well, it worked. I can't think of a more romantic place. There are not enough *oo*s in smooth, Mr. Reina. You sure know to wow us ladies!"

The next day, we went to the Uffizi museum, which houses just about every great Italian artist who stroked a canvas, entire floors featuring one artist at a time. Next lesson: Hire a guide. No way to understand what the respective artist was expressing in his work.

The museum took the better part of the day. We later stumbled into Buca dell' Orafo for lunch, a tiny *osteria* near the Ponte Vecchio, undoubtedly the most famous bridge in Italy, and had incredible pasta.

We strolled across the bridge over the famed Arno River onto the other side and visited the older part of the city and circled down a street and got lost for a while but, eventually ended up crossing another bridge over the river and found ourselves in front of the Ferragamo store. Laurie said, "Can we go in?" We did, and only in Italy does the artistry of that country show its incredible design talent. They should charge to enter and see the space, the quality, the color, and style of the merchandise was magnificent.

The merchandise was displayed to perfection. Every piece of clothing was well-coordinated. It was as if a great artist had painted it. And each department was chaperoned by a salesperson dressed like they had just stepped out of a fashion magazine.

To say nothing of the building itself. It was truly extraordinary.

We both vowed to return and spend more time on the next trip. Another lesson: Do not try to visit too many cities on any trip. You miss too much on the road. No more than three in a two-week trip. Even if you have been to those cities. We missed seeing Michelangelo's David. Not enough time, nor did we realize we needed reservations for entry.

Milano

On Saturday, Laurie and I departed for Milano for a meeting with the people from Superga. I was dreading what problems were in store for me. We took the train, and I made a mental note of how convenient it was to go from downtown in one city to the city center in the next town without having to deal with traffic and trying to find a parking place.

We checked into the historic Gallia Hotel located directly across from the monumental train station built by Mussolini after he took control of Italy in the twenties.

We had dinner that night at Antico Trattoria della Pesa. It was like eating in my sister Josie's basement. The food was prepared with the same love. Our family gatherings usually totaled thirty-six of us, and Josie and Joe would cook for two days, preparing ravioli and baking pastry and homemade bread.

The waiter brought a small plate of great bite-size veal meatballs to the table and took our wine order.

Laurie said, "My God, Joe, I have never tasted anything like this. Can we ask for seconds?" After we sipped our wine and ate the second dish of meatballs; Laurie ordered fusilli alla erbe. Easy for me to remember because over the years, she has always ordered the same pasta. For dessert, we had the best apple tarte tatin in this world. Once again, no memory problem here because we have been eating at that restaurant every time we visited Milano for the last twenty-nine years. The menu listed the opening date of the restaurant, 1880, and as I had been doing the entire trip, I used my credit card to pay for everything and took business cards from every establishment where we stayed and ate. Later when we returned to Chicago and received my credit card statement, I sat and recorded on a separate page for each city all the pertinent information and have followed this procedure every year since.

On Monday, I met with the CEO of Superga and was pleased to learn there were no issues and signed a new agreement.

That afternoon, we took a taxi to the famous Via Monte Napoleone, window shopped, and by accident stumbled into a courtyard and found a dreamlike restaurant for lunch called Il Salumaio.

After lunch, we walked to the Galleria, the first indoor shopping mall in the world built in 1878. It was the most incredible facility we had seen to date. I had never been there. It was bombed in World War II, and after the war, it was rebuilt using the original plans. Think about that for a moment, how many countries keep plans for a building for seventy years, but then the Colosseum has stood for 2,000 years, many churches for over 1,000 years.

Laurie's architectural brain was in overdrive. "Joe, I have been involved in the design and construction of some very interesting buildings in my twelve years as an architect. Having studied structure in school, I marvel at how they built this building. It would not be that difficult today with the equipment we have, but this was built when there were no machines to reach these ceiling heights. I am baffled at how they got the stained glass up there plus all the material to support it." This is another amazing discovery about this country!

We had an espresso and continued to marvel at the structure of art we were experiencing.

After our coffee, we walked across the street and stood spellbound while looking up at the Duomo di Milano. Here I was in Milano, standing in front of this beautiful church that brought me back to St. Louis, the patron saint of Milano is St. Ambrose.

It was coming home. The majority of the Italians who settled in the area of St. Louis known as The Hill were from the Milano area, and when they built the church there in 1928, it was only natural to name it St. Ambrose. The only way to describe it is through the photo at the end of this section.

We went in and found it to be even more beautiful than the duomo in Firenze.

Our plan was to walk to the next thing on our bucket list to see *l'Ultima Cena*, Leonardo da Vinci's *Last Supper*. It was a good walk, more extended than indicated on the map we had.

We learned another important lesson. For when we arrived, we were told, "You must have reservations." I tried in vain to explain we were leaving the following day. Sadly we were forced to keep it on the list for the next trip.

Lake Como

We had no idea how to get to the lake and learned the hard way. We hired a driver, which was not bad. He took us door to door to our hotel. We had asked the concierge to make arrangements for the driver. It was expensive (another lesson). That concierge got his cut.

We checked into the Hotel Metropole for two nights. While we had reservations there, we had none for dinner.

We unpacked and began walking the town. We searched for restaurants and started checking out menus. Some had both Italian and English translations, and my good memory clicked in, and I began to memorize the various main courses.

A restaurant named La Colombetta showed great promise, minimal menu, open for dinner only, and we made a note and ultimately ventured into a very nice *osteria* and had a plate of pasta and a glass of wine for lunch. We walked the entire area in and around the hotel and enjoyed a day of peace and tranquility.

We spent the rest of the afternoon relaxing by the pool at the hotel. That night, we had dinner at La Colombetta. It was so good we made reservations for the next night. It went into my book.

On Friday morning, we took the hydrofoil to Bellagio and spent the day just strolling the streets of that picturesque, beautiful city. It seemed like something out of a different world, another planet. The people were peaceful and happy as if there were no problems in their world. They were not affected by what was going on in any way, especially the economy. There were no financial problems, unemployment, or crime. The town sits right on that beautiful lake. Plenty of fish, fresh vegetables, and fruit. They were living the dream.

We stepped into a fruit and vegetable market and bought ripe figs that were dripping of juice that necessitated eating them with a napkin. Some grapes seemed like they were picked that morning. Later we walked into a cheese store and bought small cuts of three different kinds of cheese and sat in a park and consumed them with the grapes. Being with Laurie, I forgot about the problems I was facing regarding the situation with Sensi. I made up my mind. We are going to come back to this country every year for the rest of our lives.

We had a driver take us to Milano Sunday afternoon and had dinner back at Antica Trattoria della Pesa again. The next morning, we flew back to Chicago to face the problems of reorganizing Sensi and the bank debt.

St. Francis Cathedral in Assisi

Temple of Minerva in Assisi

Cantinetta Verrazzano focaccia

Cantinetta Verrazzano in Florence

Colosseum in Rome, compliments of Dave Phillips

Duomo di Milano in Milan, compliments of Dave Phillips

Fountain of Trevi in Rome, compliments of Dave Phillips

Painting of Positano, Italy

Pantheon ceiling in Rome, compliments of Dave Phillips

Pantheon exterior in Rome, compliments of Dave Phillips

Piazza Navona, Fountain of four rivers by Bernini, Rome

Piazza Navona, Rome, Bernini's statute ready to catch Borromini's church

Ponte Vecchio in Florence, Italy

CHAPTER 2

Dealing with
the Dilemmas

The minute I returned to Chicago, I made the arrangement to send Sensi a check for the money owed. That just about depleted the accounts receivable at our factor, leaving $260,000 there for operating expense. I had the boys in the warehouse inventory the sandals. I knew it was futile to try to move any product at that time of the year. But the 40,000 pairs in Assisi was ever present on my mind. There were over 40,000 of the same colors in our warehouse!

In October, I received a phone call from my loan officer at the bank. He wanted an audience with his boss and me. They came out the next day, and the boss issued a stern lecture regarding the other dilemma, the $1.1M I owed. He wanted a plan as to how I intended to reduce the loan that had remained stagnant for close to a year.

I explained the circumstances regarding the former partner, the surprise invoice due for Sensi, and that it was the end of the season; too late to move the old inventory. He did not hear a word I said. He was belligerent, pointed his finger at me, and said, "I want that plan from you in one week on how you're going to reduce this debt!"

I was right back at him. "Are you calling my note? Because if you are, you are going to find yourself in the sandal business. And by the way, don't you ever point your finger at me again. Heed this warning. I grew up in a different neighborhood than you. I promise you a Sicilian lesson you will never forget!"

I had lunch the next day with a friend Tony Cascino, and he sensed my concerns, and I shared them with him. He knew the background and success we had had with the sandals. I told him my plan to rebuild the company and then sell it. He asked, "How much was the former partner originally going to pay you for your third of the company?" I told him $250,000. He responded, "I would like to buy that third. Will you take $250,000?" I was in shock.

We concluded the deal the very next morning in his office with our attorneys. Then I went straight to the bank and gave them a check for $200,000!

In November, I drove to Madison, Wisconsin, and met with the shoe buyer for Famous Footwear. They had stores all over the country. I sold her 80,000 pairs of sandals, those in my warehouse and those in Assisi in the Sensi facility for $5 a pair. Our cost was $1.25. She wanted them shipped in January. I faxed a copy of the purchase order to my loan officer so that he could shove it in the face of his boss.

I have long believed that there's a large book somewhere in the sky with a page for every day of life. The Tony Cascino page was a significant one, as was the order from Famous Footwear.

In early January, the night before a trade show in Orlando, Florida, I met Tony for dinner at his Florida winter home. At dinner, he said, "You are a different person today than you were last September." I laughed and said, "You had a lot to do with that, Tony."

My mind was racing. All I could think of was my mom, her determination in resolving problems, her work ethic, and how I inherited it. Three months had passed since the meeting with the bank, and the $1.1M loan had dropped $600,000! My sister Josie's logic interrupted my thoughts of mom. My personality surfaced next. I was undeterred, determined to relaunch Sensi. What was driving me? I needed to prove to my former partner what a fool he was to let me get away, to make him realize that I had been the driving force in marketing our business. But then again, he didn't give a damn about all this. Why waste time thinking about him?

I thanked Tony for his trust and belief in me and promised his investment was in me, not the sandal.

The very first morning at the fair, I was approached by Peter Link, the VP of product development for the Deckers sandal company. He had one of our sandal soles sliced in half. He explained that when permeated with salt or muddy water, his product smelled and asked if we could make a sole with our drainage system for his sandal.

At this point, I was looking for any port in the storm and replied yes.

He asked, "How much?" I told him probably two to three dollars. He suggested, "Can we meet at the Action Sport Show in San Diego the following week? I want you to meet my boss, Doug Otto." We agreed to meet for lunch on Saturday.

Laurie joined me for the trip and watched our show booth while Peter, Doug, and I had lunch.

Doug said, "I used to see your sandal in every store up and down the state of California, but the presence has diminished. What happened?"

I explained the situation regarding my partner's moving the company's direction to gifts and accessories and how he released the shoe sales force and replaced them with accessory salespeople to sell everything. "I am going to hire a new sales force and build it back, and then I plan to sell it."

"Do you want to sell it to us?"

I laughed. "No. Let me build it, and then I will come calling on you."

Doug asked, "Where are you going after the show?"

"I am heading to Palm Springs for a few days."

"Why don't you drive up to Santa Barbara and come see our operation for a day?"

We agreed and returned to the show.

On Monday, we visited his factory, had lunch, and talked about his business. He had twenty salespeople and sold fine specialty stores and was doing a little over $5M in sales. He expected to double the revenue for 1991.

We had a nice dinner that night and agreed to stay in touch, and the next morning Laurie and I drove to Palm Springs. Late that afternoon, Doug called and said, "Peter and I would like to drive over and talk to you." They stayed at my house that night, and we discussed several options on how we could get together and help each other with product development and marketing.

The next morning, we agreed to do a fifty-fifty joint venture, where I would assume the role as president and national sales manager, use their twenty salespeople, and work with Laurie and Peter on product development. Doug wanted a buy and sell agreement as part of the deal. Part of the agreement was that his company would assume all administration, financial, sales promotion, warehousing, and shipping. We agreed to start with $50,000 each. My end was the current inventory in my warehouse, so I went into the deal with no cash investment.

By the end of the next week, we signed the document prepared by his attorney. The contract stipulated that I would receive $0.75 a pair for every pair we purchased each year for bringing the license and product to the table as long as we were in business. The buyout was based on five times the net profit the previous year, with a minimum of $1,000,000 cash for our half of the venture.

Once again, the large book in the sky surfaced. Another page turned.

In February and March, I traveled with all twenty of Deckers' sales reps and went on calls with them. We sold just about every one of their accounts, mostly test orders, and this convinced both Doug and Peter that this was a good move for both firms.

In late March, Laurie and I departed for Rome to learn color direction and search for ideas for new sandal designs. We stayed at the famed Inghilterra Hotel. We took our favorite walk to the Trevi Fountain, threw three coins in, went on to the Pantheon, stopped for pizza, and proceeded to Piazza Navona. Laurie said, "You always pay for everything. It is my turn. Let's have a glass of wine. We have been going nonstop since we got off the airplane."

That night, we went to Campo de Fiore for the first time. I had read about a seafood restaurant called Hosteria del Pesce. We were both surprised when we arrived, for there was this huge cart stocked with live fresh fish, shrimp, lobster, clams, and mussels!

We were seated immediately. I had learned early on to be sure to arrive on time for reservations, and they served us a small dish of baby shrimp that had been sautéed in butter and garlic that was to die for. We ordered a bottle of Cervaro white wine. I had trouble reading the list and determined I needed to learn Italian wines.

The next day, we walked to the Forum and later to the top overlooking a series of columns below us. Laurie bet me she could toss a coin and land it on the flat top of one. We both tried one and did not come close. She tried a second as did I, and this time, we both landed one. We agreed to renew this another time because she had another coin and I did not. She tossed hers anyway and missed.

That night, we decided to try another restaurant I had read about, Al Passetto. It was a beautiful ristorante that was a tradition in Rome. Most of the patrons were locals, and it went into my book.

The next day, we took a taxi to the Trastevere area of Rome and just walked, checked out the shops, and had lunch in the courtyard of Cafe Romolo, located via Porta Settimiana 8. The menu cover was a copy of a painting by famous artist Joan Miro. I spoke to the owner of the restaurant after noticing more of Miro's works of art on the walls.

She told me that Miro sketched there in his early days and would leave the sketches in payment for food and wine.

We had pasta con asparagi (asparagus) with a carafe of white house wine. Laurie said, "I don't know why you spend the money for the best wines when we can order house wines that are this good."

There's a story about that restaurant building. While Michelangelo was painting the Sistine Chapel, he took a break one day and rode his donkey to visit his friend Raphael, who was living above the building with his mistress. But Raphael was not there, he left a note with a piece of chalk on the wall, "I missed you." If only those walls could talk, what stories would unfold?

We departed for Assisi the next morning by train, and Giampiero Sensi picked us up at the train station and my concern about the language problem was for naught. Lorenzo had asked his niece Laura Bonci, who was working on her master's degree in English, to join us for two days. She made our work a delight.

Laurie had jumped into the development process, first by being in the factory working with the plant manager Lionello, who did not speak English. But somehow, she learned the technical process of sandal construction. I worked the business end in the office.

Laurie had contacted a color forecasting company in New York and sent for color selections that came in small yarn balls. The Sensis were impressed with how fast she gravitated to everything. That evening we were invited to dinner at the family home. We were served homemade pasta with a very light cream sauce mixed with parmigiano, appetizer-sized portions. I read Laurie's mind. I knew she wished it could be the main course. Later, fresh vegetables were served with veal cutlets and a second meat dish. Laurie asked what it was and was advised it was a pigeon. Again I read her mind. She called pigeons flying rats. We passed on the pigeon.

We stayed at the Hotel Savoy, which at best was a two-star hotel, not one of my favorites. A two-star hotel is similar to a Motel Six, bare-bones, a bed, usually an old tub, rarely a shower, worn towels, never a face cloth. I had paid my dues in those types of hotels as a kid when I first went on the road with The Arrow shirt company in the sixties.

The following day after breakfast, we walked up to the piazza Minerva and stumbled into a small hotel called Umbra and asked to see a room. It was much nicer than the Savoy. The rooms were larger, had a shower and large new bath towels. It was clean, and they had a lovely dining room. I took a card.

We went to lunch at a very nice little *osteria* and were both astounded at the way the Sensis ate. First a pasta dish, then a meat dish, usually with potatoes or a fresh vegetable, wine with every meal, and finished with an espresso. Laurie tried to order a cappuccino, and Mr. Sensi stopped it and explained it is not a good idea to have hot milk after a meal. Cappuccino only in the morning. We follow that advice to this day.

We finished the afternoon by being dropped off for a visit at St. Francis church and departed for Rome the next day. That last night, we stayed at the Inghilterra and had dinner at Babette on via Margutta in the outdoor garden. It was a delightful evening, and we later strolled to the Piazza di Spagna and talked about how short the trip was. We vowed next time to take at least a whole week to travel one of the seven regions and to do so each time we return.

The hotel ordered a car to take us to the airport the next morning, and we liked the lady driver. I took her card and tipped her well. She was a single mom and promised we would have her pick us up at the airport on our next trip. We also learned it was less expensive than the taxi fare. She later stopped driving and gave us the name of a colleague, Antonio, who we use today.

On Sunday, March 25, my mother passed away at age ninety-seven. It was sudden. She woke up Friday morning not feeling well and was taken to the hospital, and I received the call from my sister, Josie, late Sunday afternoon, and she died in my arms Monday afternoon. It was the end of an era, but in my heart, I was at peace, for she was in constant pain with arthritis and could not get more than an hour's sleep at night, sometimes sleeping on her knees with her head on the side of the bed. We did not speak. I saw in her eyes she was ready. I was the last family member in the room. My times with her on our memorable trips flashed before my mind. I walked out of the room in tears, and the rest of the family went in to pay their respects. Mom missed our wedding by two weeks. We were married April 7. The wedding and reception was held at the Bellevue Club, courtesy of our dear friend Jane Silvestri. The weather was perfect. We had fifty friends and relatives and a very nice three-piece band.

In June, I attended the Deckers sales meeting and introduced the current Sensi line, and met the new vice president of sales, Ron Page. He had hired a sales group for California, Tom Seavey, and my old Sensi rep from Texas, Don Campbell. Don and I were good friends. We had an enjoyable two days together, and my excitement about the turnaround in six months was only exceeded by the fact the loan at the bank was down to $450,000, and I could breathe.

My real estate investments in the two buildings that we had under construction were flourishing. Sensi sales for the year far exceeded our projections, and we showed a very nice profit for the season. We purchased 260,000 pairs, which exceeded projections by

10,000, so the company owed us $195,000. When it hit our bank, I had them reduce the debt by the entire amount.

I called Peter Link and explained we needed to go to Assisi in September to develop the line for 1992, and we agreed to go right after Labor Day. I explained the drill, to meet in Rome on a Sunday to shop for ideas and plan on going to Assisi on Tuesday for two days. Laurie and I planned on going our way for a trip afterward for ten days. I invited him to join us in Firenze afterward. I made all the arrangements for hotels and restaurants and asked Lorenzo to have Laura Bonci join us.

Once we arrived in Assisi, we checked into the Hotel Umbra and showed Peter the town, and the next morning, Giampiero picked us up and took us to the factory. At the time, Birkenstock sandals were hot, and we designed a new double strap sandal that resembled their product. Ours was forty percent cheaper and incorporated the Sensi patented drainage system. We called it LaJolla. For the record, Sensi used all our colors and new designs for European consumption. That night, we took Peter to La Pallotta for dinner, and he could not believe the prices, which included a bottle of local wine. We ate for just under $35. He also loved the old town area where we stayed. He said, "I have to bring my family here. What a pleasant hideaway."

We took the train the next day to Firenze and checked into the hotel Savoy. We had dinner reservations at Ottorino, family-owned and operated with the father cooking in the kitchen and other family members were serving. We ordered fiori di zucca (the flower that grows at the top of the zucchini plant) for an appetizer. The farmers in this country throw it away when they cut it from the plant, but not in Italy. In some restaurants, they stuff it sometimes with cheese or anchovies, bathe it in a flour and egg wash and deep fry it. It was a first for us, and Laurie said, "I could make a meal out of this."

The following day, we had reservations to see Michelangelo's David, and after a short line, we were allowed into the building and were amazed at the size of the statue and found it hard to believe it has stood since the sixteenth century! I have quite an imagination, but standing in front of this incredible treasure, I tried to visualize

Michelangelo traveling to Carrara to oversee the excavation of this immense piece of marble, then getting it down the side of a mountain in one piece. Next, lifting it onto some wagon and hauling it to Firenze. And having the patience and perseverance to create the masterpiece.

We spent the next part of the day once again going to the Uffizi museum. Another lesson: there is no way to see and observe it in one trip.

The next day, we visited Michelangelo's home and studio. It was plain and simple. It is in a beautiful area very close to the city center. The rooms were tiny and had very few windows. It was hard to imagine someone of his stature living in these meager surroundings. We tried to imagine him designing his statues in his small office, but the most impressive thing was that it was still there, as if he was away for a few days, except the few days were 350 years! That night, we returned to Buca dell' Orafo for dinner.

Our exploration of the city took us to Fiesole, a small town overlooking the city. The views were spectacular. It was quaint, typical of so many small towns we had visited. It had clean, small homes and I tried to imagine life there during Michelangelo's time, wondering what it must have been like, thinking of all the great artists living there in the sixteenth century. We saw the ancient amphitheater, the ancient church, and one of the most beautiful parks either of us had ever seen. We had lunch at a tiny *trattoria*, very simple with a half carafe of vino rosso, and we had a plate of pasta with marinara sauce and could not believe it cost less than twelve dollars! We finished lunch and took the bus back to the area where we boarded it. That afternoon, we walked to Palazzo Pitti, which was built in the latter part of the fifteenth century by Luca Pitti as his palazzo. Later in the early part of the sixteenth century, the Medici family purchased it. In the seventeenth century, it housed King Victor Emmanuel when Firenze was the capital of Italy. Once again, we were astonished it was still in existence in this incredible location. Another tribute to that great city. Next, we visited the Basilica di San Lorenzo. We closed the day at the beautiful Boboli Gardens and marveled at how the Italians have maintained all the treasures we had visited for centuries.

We departed Firenze sadly. Once again, we had that tremendous need to return, vowing never to come to Italy without spending a few days there. I told Laurie, "Next time we come here, let's stay a week." Laurie and I took the train to Milano for two days before returning to Chicago.

Once again, we checked into the Gallia. We were beginning to be recognized, and they treated us royally. We were upgraded to a superior room and treated to a bottle of Prosecco (Italian sparkling wine) and had a beautiful bowl of fresh fruit in the room. And while we were unpacking, there was a knock on the door. Laurie answered and returned with a plate of three different kinds of cheese. That night, we had dinner reservations at Antica Trattoria Della Pesa. Here too, we were welcomed back. This time, the same server, as in the past, knew better than to bring us the usual four meatballs. He brought us eight.

The next morning, we came prepared. We had reservations to go to the church Santa Maria Della Grazie. A special room that is thermostatically controlled housed *L'Ultima Cena*, Leonardo da Vinci's *Last Supper*. The surprise is when you enter. There is a small photo of the other fresco in the room. At the far end is Giovanni Donato's crucifixion. He did the fresco in the fifteenth century. The photo is the original church where he painted it. It was accidentally destroyed by Allied bombers during World War II. Milan was a major industrial city supplying Germany and Italy with war materials. That church was totally destroyed. It was rubble, except for the one wall, the wall now sitting opposite Da Vinci's marvel. We were astounded at the enormity of the *Last Supper*, approximately fifteen feet high and thirty feet long. Almost the exact size of Donato's masterpiece of Jesus and the other two men on the cross on each side of Christ.

Only twenty-five of us were allowed in the room. A woman was in the process of restoring the *Last Supper*. It was partially finished, and she estimated it would take her twenty years to complete the project. I told Laurie, "Every time we come to Milan, remind me to make reservations to watch her progress." What an amazing experience, sitting in a room with two incredible objects of art dating back to the fifteenth century. Using a little imagination, we were viewing

Thursday nights Passover Seder and Friday afternoon's crucifixion of Jesus Christ!

I said to Laurie as we exited, "How do we top this?"

We flew back to Chicago, content that we achieved our goals for the trip.

CHAPTER 3

1992

Laurie and I departed Chicago nonstop for Rome in March to spend two days searching the shoe market for style and color ideas for the Sensi line. We stayed at the Inghilterra and strolled the Via Condotti and several boutiques in the area. There are many shoe stores of all types. The Via Condotti has the top designer brands, such as Ferragamo and Prada, the streets on both sides of it have casual and dress shoe stores for both genders.

We made our way for the short walk to our favorite sites, the fountain of Trevi and the Pantheon, and we stopped for the traditional slice of pizza on the way to Piazza Navona. An artist was sketching the piazza, and at the time, his attention was at Bernini's fountain. I remarked, "What a thrill it must be for this guy to be in this incredible city using his talent to spend time going from famous sites and using his creativity making a living."

Laurie said, "Isn't that what we do? We get to visit here once or twice a year, using our talents to create sandals, and go to the trade shows marketing our talents to make a living."

"Listen to the Greek philosopher!"

The sun was bright and dominated the blue sky, not a cloud to be seen. The water bouncing off the statues in the fountains brought them to life. It was a perfect day for the artists who were painting and displaying their finished work for sale.

That night, we decided to try a new restaurant for dinner, Da Bolognese, and walked to the Piazza del Popolo located near the Flaminia gate, which in early Rome was the main entrance to the city. Even though it is a short walk to the Piazza di Spagna, we had never been to that piazza. We could not believe the statues on the street. They were massive; beautiful white marble intricately carved works of art!

The sun was starting to set, and they almost seemed like they could talk. What a sight. The piazza was huge. Kudos to the Italians for keeping the piazzas all through Italy and how they refrained from destroying them and building condos and commercial buildings in them. Many museums would be proud to have those works of art.

We had a delightful dinner, starting with prosciutto con melon, then spaghetti Bolognese, and finished with insalata mista. We were told by our waiter, who spoke a little English, that the food was very typical of Bologna. He told us we must visit his city. With no modesty, he said, "The food in Bologna was far superior to Rome." I made a mental note to put that famous city on our bucket list.

The next day, we continued our exploration of Rome. I had read about the Baths of Caracalla established in 216 AD. The engineering of the Italians, their genius of bringing water from the aqueducts ten to fourteen miles away. They were able to heat enough water to bathe 10,000 people a day! It took archeologists, in their study of Rome, over two thousand years to figure out how they were able to heat that water. During a dig in Turkey, they unearthed a Roman bath dating back to the fourth century in near perfect condition. Those were the same baths built by the Romans when they controlled the country under Constantine the Great. They were wood fire heated under the floors below clay tiles under the water in a unique way. Here we were, tourists 1,800 years later and could not imagine the undertaking by the Romans making this happen. These were the smaller of the two baths used by the Romans. They were started by Emperor Severus about AD 212. Caracalla's father believed the Romans as a people smelled terrible. Caracalla (formally known as

Marcus Aurelius Anthony) finished the baths. There are many rooms used for various activities, including massage and sports programs. A caste system prevailed as to use of the facilities. Another amazing thing about Rome, the location and size made the real estate value of the baths unimaginable.

We walked back to the Spanish Steps. Every tourist that has ever been to those famous steps has taken a photo of them. Few know the history. They are below the Trinita dei Monti church and were constructed in the eighteenth century by an Italian architect. The Spanish embassy sits in the piazza, and they were built to give access to the church for the embassy. The cost was provided by a wealthy French patron. There is a sign on a building just to the right of the fountain in the center of the piazza that states John Keats once lived there. Sadly, McDonald's opened a burger restaurant next to that building.

It was a warm, calm evening, and as always, we were happy to be alive, enjoying a Saturday in what was fast becoming our favorite city.

The next day, we walked to the Colosseum to renew our contest, tossing coins in an attempt to land one on top of the columns. We had no luck. Neither of us scored.

It was one of those days with no schedule, bright and sunny, and we opted to taxi to Campo de Fiore for a casual lunch. We later had trouble finding a cab and walked across the street in the direction of the city center and unknowingly strolled directly to the Piazza Navona. What a sight and surprise. By a stroke of luck, we stumbled on our favorite piazza.

Laurie looked at me and said, "What are you, Christopher Columbus?" I reminded her, "We prefer to call him by his Italian name Colombo." The usual throngs of tourists were there, and we made a mental note that we can walk to Campo de Fiore in the future instead of the long taxi ride.

That night, we opted to go for a casual dinner a few blocks from the hotel, till this day one of our favorites, Toto la Cucina di Roma on Via Carrozze. I had read about it in *Travel and Leisure* magazine, and the food lived up to the article. It is a few blocks from Piazza di Spagna.

On Monday, we took the train to Assisi, and Giampiero Sensi picked us up. With our broken Italian, we convinced him to take us to a store where we could buy a shower curtain. The tub at the hotel Umbra did not have one. Every time we took a shower, we flooded the bathroom floor.

The hotel owner got a kick out of the shower curtain and commented on how considerate we were. She said they would take it down after we departed and put it up for our next stay. We dropped our luggage in the room and proceeded to the factory to work on the 1993 line. The three of us had a coffee at Bar Sensi.

When we arrived at the factory, Mr. Sensi's niece, Laura Bonci, was already there.

Laurie took charge, working with Giampiero and Maria Grazie and Laura on the new line, while I spent time with Lorenzo and a charming bookkeeper on projections for 1992 sales.

Tuesday morning, we went to Bar Sensi (no relation to the Sensis) for coffee and great pastry, and later, Giampiero picked us up and took us to the factory to continue working on the new line.

Lorenzo thanked us for the 1991 orders. He shipped slightly over 250,000 pairs. I didn't share the fact that it put $195,000 into my company, which went straight to pay down the bank loan, which had moved to LaSalle Bank.

We had a light dinner at the hotel and packed to be ready for an early train ride the next morning for Firenze.

When we stepped off the train, our awe of that city returned like the first visit. I again had trouble believing I was actually there. I would occasionally drift back to lunches with the merchandise manager at Carson's, my Arrow client back in the late sixties. His name was Ed Bergeson, and once a year, he would go to Firenze for buying meetings with the corporate buying office for the store. He would relate his experiences, sites, and restaurants. I made it a priority to always take him to lunch when he returned from those trips, vowing to go there. At the time, it was out of the question. There was no money to go to Italy. I was struggling to make ends meet with three kids.

We had put together what sites we intended to visit and a side trip to Lucca, supposedly the home of best olive oil in all of Italy. We walked via Tornabuoni, which extends from Antinori Square to ponte (bridge), Santa Trinita. This is the fashion street of Firenze, and the finest designers of all of Italy have shops there. It truly is a pleasure to stroll, strong competition to the Via Condotti in Rome, and Via Monte Napoleone in Milano. We then walked to the Piazza Della Repubblica and stopped at Caffe Gilli, the coffee shop across from the famous Savoy hotel, and had an espresso and a piece of pastry. My fascination with that city has never ceased to amaze me.

That night, we went to Taverna Bronzino for dinner, another great meal, always consistent, regardless of what we ate. We learned it was the former home of Branzino, whose real name was Agnolo di Cosimo. He was a sixteenth-century painter who worked in the court of Medici, the most powerful and the wealthiest family of Tuscany. One might say, "All right, another famous artist," but we found it interesting that here on a very narrow street we would call an alley, dining in his home that dated nearly 500 years. It was still there, and we were told the home was almost the exact way it was when he lived there; that the city insisted that living spaces of important people could not be altered.

We took an early train to Lucca the next morning, and when we arrived, we were amazed at the twenty-foot brick wall that surrounded the city. We walked across the street from the train station to an underground tunnel that went under the wall and found ourselves in what appeared to be the tenth century. That brick wall was so well-preserved it seemed like it had been built the previous year.

We strolled to the Piazza Napoleone and had a coffee to check my notes on what to see. There are numerous towers, best remembered as tributes to competitions among wealthy families. The higher the structure, the more notoriety. We walked to what I had noted as the highest, the Torre delle Ore (tower of the clock) and Laurie pushed me to walk to the top. By the time we got up there, I needed a shot of oxygen, but the view of the valley so captivated me I stopped complaining. Olive trees as far as the eye could see, it was like stars blanketing the sky on a perfectly clear night.

My notes showed the town dated before Christ was born, and the high walls were constructed to hold off attackers during the city wars. It dated back to the Etruscans.

We soon found ourselves in a vast piazza that was once an amphitheater, with a series of shops and caffes. I did not have any restaurants on my notes, but we stumbled on a quaint place, Da Pasquale, and checked the menu. By now, I had no problem reading and translating the menu, and we decided to give it a try. Sitting on the table was a bottle of house Chianti wine and a bottle of the greenest olive oil we had ever seen. Neither had a label. A waiter brought a huge basket with three hunks of crusty bread and a plate. He poured olive oil on it and then motioned to dip the bread. Only in Italy. The ristorante name went into my book. We took a casual walk around the town and agreed to visit it again. One must remember that the town as it appears today dates back to the ninth century. The streets were laid out for horses and wagons and carriages. They are too narrow for autos and contain shops with housing above. They do, however, provide means of leading to all the main piazzas.

Laurie said, "It is amazing how many towns like this exist in this country. The people are so cool everywhere we visit." I agreed and reiterated, "That's why I want to do each region one at a time. I don't want to miss any of them."

We took the five o'clock train back to Firenze and had a glass of wine at the hotel.

That night, we had dinner at Ottorino, and Giorgio, the owner, greeted us and seated us at our favorite table and, within minutes, returned with a huge platter of *fiore di zucca* (deep-fried flowers of zucchini). Later we walked up to the gelato shop Perche No, across from Cantinetta di Verrazzano, and had supposedly the best in the city.

The next morning, we departed by train for Milano. We arrived and checked into the Galli, where we once again were upgraded to a superior room and found the bottle of Prosecco and fresh fruit in the room.

I was well-prepared for this city. We had reservations to return to see the progress of the restoration of the *The Last Supper* that afternoon and were amazed at the improvement from the previous visit.

I had been reading the history of Italy since the unification in 1861 by General Garibaldi, who was outmaneuvered by the duke of Cavour, a very serious statesman. It had become a political movement among all the states. The real name of Cavour was Camillo Benso, and he led the group to the unification, which also included Sicily. Sicily, at the time, was controlled by Naples, and Garibaldi gets credit for rescuing them and bringing them to the unification.

Part of our plan was to see Pinacoteca di Brera, a fine art gallery, which had been a palazzo, later converted to a convent. It houses the great art of Raphael, Rubens' *Last Supper*, the famous *Magi* by Correggio is a must-see when visiting Milano.

That night, we took a forty-minute cab ride to a Michelin star ristorante I had read about in *Departures* magazine called Aimo and Nadia, and we had the dinner of the trip. It holds a top spot in my book on where to eat in Milano. There are no words to describe the food.

We concluded our trip and departed for Chicago the next morning. We always flew American Airlines. I would be remiss if I failed to give credit to my friend Ralph Richardi for always finding seats for us at the last minute in business class. He remains a good friend to this day.

We flew to Chicago and continued working on our various real estate developments. The sales reports on Sensi were great, and we placed reorders with the factory.

I set up trips with the Deckers' reps for six weeks in April and May, traveled to Florida for two days, and called on both small and large stores. The goal was not only to sell but to teach the salespeople and, in many cases, their sub reps how to pitch Sensi my way. It was to be a confidence boost for them because we never took no for an answer. In many cases, these stores had never heard of Sensi. And we were getting back into previous accounts that had not purchased it in a couple of years. We were asked, "What happened to you people? We bought the line for five years, and then no one called on us!"

Sensi was a good mix with their other products. Due to the success they were having with Teva, Simple, and Ugg, they opened the doors for us, and I knew the deal with Doug was the right move.

In June 1992, I received a call from Doug at the end of the season, and he offered to buy our fifty percent of Sensi USA for the agreed price in the contract, $1,000,000. In addition, a settlement was decided on the amount due on the sandal purchases for 1992, which brought the total for the $0.75 per pair royalty to $200,000!

Another page in that book upstairs. We concluded the deal in two weeks. And as soon as the money was transferred to LaSalle Bank, I paid off the loan balance on the original $450,000 loan. It took less than two years from that disastrous day in 1990 in the Sensi office for the comeback.

Laurie, early on, said, "I don't know how you sleep nights." I replied, "Who says I sleep?"

Tony Cascino was overwhelmed at what had transpired, and he and Lorayne took us to dinner, and he paid us a supreme compliment. "Joe Reina, where do we go from here? I would like to roll over my share of the money I am getting plus my original investment, wherever you want to go with it." We thanked them for the compliment and dinner and told him I would get back to him on the possible reinvestment. He later received a check for $500,000, which doubled his investment.

CHAPTER 4

1993 Trips with the Moccas and Mike Reina

G rowing up in my old neighborhood, we all fell into one category: the middle class. There were a few families that had arrived at the table of success, but one could count them on one hand.

But by the early sixties, people from the area began traveling abroad. My mom went back to Sicily in 1959 and spent three months. She began encouraging all of us to go. My sister, Josie, didn't hesitate, and she and Joe started taking a trip every other year. Joe took many photos, and we would sit around the dinner table in their kitchen and listen to all the stories.

They had never been to Greece. Neither Laurie nor I had been there. I called Josie and discussed a trip and she jumped right on it. I firmly believed she and Joe kept a bag packed, ready to head to the airport at the drop of a hat, especially if it included Europe.

In September, we flew to Rome and met up with and her and Joe, and later we flew to Athens for two nights. I had the sites lined up, and the first place we visited was the impressive Parthenon, later the Acropolis and Acropolis Museum. On the second day, we went to the Herod Atticus Odeon. The sites were especially significant for Laurie. Greece is her homeland, but Josie, who had read so many world history books was just as excited and impressed. She had to abort her high school education after one semester to do the household chores because my mom was the only one of six of us working in the middle of the Great Depression.

We lived across the street from the public library, and she read two or three books a week. Her favorites were history, both American and world. Her imagination would wander. She would find herself in all the great cities of the world, never even dreaming of visiting them, and here she was.

Laurie ordered for us at restaurants. Josie and Joe knew nothing about Greek food. We had Pastitsio, baked pasta, Moussaka, a baked eggplant and potato dish with béchamel sauce, Dolmades, grape leaves stuffed with rice and ground beef. For dessert, we had baklava, phyllo dough layers stuffed with chopped nuts and honey, and robust Greek coffee called Ellinikous. We agreed the food was great everywhere, not as good as our mom's and grandmother's, but well worth the prices. It was abundant, usually more than we could finish.

We had a light-hearted discussion the night we had pasta. Laurie asked, "Joe, did you ever share your nephew Jimmy's article about archaeologists finding noodles in a cave in Greece dating back 5,000 years? We Greeks get credit for discovering spaghetti!"

"No. We still credit Marco Polo, who brought them back from China."

"Besides, if it is true that the Greeks first used noodles, outside of baking them, the Italians taught the world how to cook them." We all laughed.

We took a small plane to Crete and stayed two nights. We stayed in Eleonas Country Village. I had read the history of Greece and was most impressed with the lifestyle of the people, the food, and the beautiful white sands on the beach where we stayed. I chose for us to visit the Palace of Knossos, the Artifacts at Heraklion, and we walked the Samaria Gorges. We just walked the town and enjoyed the people and the food the last afternoon.

From Crete, we went to Santorini and loved it. Without a doubt, it is one of the most romantic, picturesque places in the world. It was Laurie's return to her homeland. Her grandparents on her mother's side and her grandmother on her father's side all immigrated.

The first day, we just walked from one end of the island to the other. The first night, we walked to Oia to view the sunset, and a miraculous thing happened. Almost as if it was planned, the minute the sun started its decline, a dead silence prevailed, and then from a rooftop a man began singing, "Return to Sorrento" a cappella. The sun glistened over the calm Aegean Sea. I thought to myself how great it was to be with Laurie, my sister, and Joe. I said, "This is a long way from The Hill where we grew up."

The next day, we went to ancient Thira to visit the archeological site, a must in a visit while in Santorini. It dates back to the ninth century BC, with ruins during the reign of Alexander the Great. They were so well-preserved it did not take a lot of imagination to visualize what life was like 2,300 years ago. We spent the last day in the village of Pyros. The whitewashed buildings with the blue domes left an indelible memory on us.

We stumbled into a gallery where I noticed a beautiful watercolor of the immediate area, including postcards of it. I asked the clerk, presumably the artist, if the painting was for sale. He replied in very limited English no. A while later, I returned to the front of the gallery to purchase what I was sure was one of his personal works of art. I finally wore him down, and he agreed to sell it to me.

We flew back to Athens and transferred to a flight to Rome, and spent the night. Josie and Joe had been to Rome and had seen the Trevi Fountain but had not spent any time at the Pantheon. Nor had they been to our other two haunts, the pizza and gelato favorites. They loved the Piazza Navona. I briefed them on the history of our three favorite sites in Rome. It was heartwarming sharing experiences with my sweetheart, my sister, and Joe. We laughed about the old days and recounted many memories together. There are four photos of her on my desk, and I see her every morning.

Then on to Positano for three days, sharing our favorite sites and restaurants. The first night was to the San Pietro and next to Donna Rosa, and we had Ravioli con Melanzane. Josie promised to make them for us next time we were in St. Louis.

Sharing the food and love of Italy with them remains one of my finest memories.

Josie looked at me and said, "Joe, can you believe this? First Greece, then Rome, and now Positano. Not in our wildest dreams when we were kids living in the three rooms behind the original grocery store could we ever have imagined taking a trip like this."

That night, I had trouble falling asleep, and my mind drifted back to my childhood and the old neighborhood. I remember at age eight collecting soda pop bottles for a month and later getting .02 a bottle, maybe totaling two dollars. And later making $.02 a newspaper on my paper route. And here we were in a hotel in Positano paying $250 a night for a room. Hard to believe. My brother Carlo's advice surfaced: "Joe, never forget where you came from."

On November 1993, I received a disturbing letter from Lorenzo Sensi, who sadly informed me Deckers had ordered only 30,000 pairs of sandals for the year, down from 250,000 the previous season.

"Giuseppe, what did you do to me?" He played to my guilt. I felt I had come out smelling like a rose the previous year, selling the company to Doug. Now, because of my love and respect for that great family, it was my turn.

I called Doug Otto but was unable to get in touch with him for months. Finally, I received a call from Ron Page, VP of sales, and we discussed what had happened. They had made a lot of mistakes, first by putting the sandal in the marketing department of a shoe accessory group that focused on selling shoe polish, shoelaces, shoeshine rags, and brushes. They dropped the ball completely. They only sold 14,000 pairs for the entire season, and Deckers was stuck with the rest of the 30,000 pairs they purchased. Ron asked if I was interested in buying back the license. I laughed and said, "There were no rubber bands on the contract I had with Doug." He responded, "Doug will be going to the Super Trade Show in Atlanta the first week of February. I will have him call you when he is back."

Soon after, Doug called me from Atlanta, and we explored ideas on how to turn the business around.

My son Michael had graduated from Arizona State University and was working for Hensley the Budweiser beer distributor in Phoenix. I called him and asked, "Would you like to go into the sandal business and handle marketing and distribution for Sensi?" His reply was an immediate yes. I explained Laurie and I were busy completing a ten-unit condominium development in Chicago, and I could only give him limited help initially.

Mike and I flew to Atlanta and cut a deal with Doug to become the sublicensor and pay him a royalty of $0.90 a pair. He agreed we could use some of his sales force until we developed our own sales team. He also agreed to let us use part of the huge Deckers show booth, which now contained their Teva sandal brand, Simple Sneakers, and Ugg. Let's say at this point, I have met many people in my fifty-seven years in the apparel industry, and Doug Otto sits at the very top of the list. He is so honest and easygoing, and it was always a pleasure to deal with him. There is not a drop of ego in his personality.

The next morning, we showed up at the trade show, and I introduced Mike to the sales force, the same people I had worked with, and one by one, we hired them for every significant territory in the country.

I learned that one of the major mistakes Deckers made was cutting the sales commission I was paying before the buyout from ten percent to five percent textbook for how to lose sales.

I made it clear that we would pay ten percent, and of course, that got everyone's attention.

Another mistake that had been made was my salesperson for Japan had been fired, and sales in Japan had also slipped.

After the show, Mike went back to Phoenix and rented a warehouse and hired a part-time administrator who knew bookkeeping and billing. He hired his old buddy Henry Killian from Chicago to run the warehouse. Henry had worked in our warehouse as a teenager, so he knew how to pick and pack orders. We made arrangements to take the Sensi inventory sitting in Deckers' warehouse. In a very short period, we were in business.

Mike started marketing the sandal with the spas in the Phoenix/ Scottsdale area. His young college graduate hire exclusively called on the spas, and he was writing orders daily. Spas were a wide open market across the country. In the past, this market had been ignored by the original Sensi team.

The spa industry was huge with its own trade shows twice a year. We joined the organization and purchased a portable show booth that could be shipped to the show and easily assembled by one person.

This was the busy part of the sandal season, and I set up a plan to travel with the Deckers sales reps, a barnstorming trip that took me to every major city in a six-week period. Business was so good; it necessitated ordering two containers of sandals, 80,000 pairs, and for the third time, Sensi rose from the ashes of Phoenix. No pun intended as we were running the business from there.

Laurie and I were bouncing a lot of balls in the air. She quit her job in the architect's office and joined a partner and me in the current condo development. Plus, I was working on the renovation of a large industrial building. Both were consuming most of my ready cash.

In April, Laurie and Mike Reina and I went to Rome and checked into Hotel Inghilterra, and spent two nights sharing the sites. Mike had never been to Italy. The plan was to go to Assisi and work on the new line for 1995 and then to spend some time in Firenze, a couple of days in Venice, and finish the trip in Milan.

In Rome, we took our favorite walk explaining a little history of it, and did the typical tourist things. We ate in our famous restaurants and shared a little history of the city. The weather in April is usually a great time to go to Italy, avoiding the crowds and the summer heat.

Next, we took the train to Assisi and had a pleasant surprise. Lorenzo's other daughter, Giovanna, had joined the company and spoke English, which again made our job more manageable. I had purchased a book on Italian/English translations of both words and phrases and started communicating with Giampiero by fax and was having no problem. I used my terrible Italian in hotels and restaurants, even though in the big cities, English was spoken. Most Italians would always smile and say, "You are from Sicily."

We finished a nice session with the Sensi family, took Mike to dinner both nights to eat at La Pallotta, and departed for Firenze the next morning.

We stayed at Loggiato Hotel and left for focaccia and watched Mike devour four pieces. We had espresso, only after Mike tried to order a cappuccino, and he got one of the early lessons about coffee in Italy.

We took him to the duomo and then to the Piazza della Signoria and later strolled to the Ponte Vecchio. After touring the areas on the other side of the Arno, we walked back to the hotel and relaxed before dinner. The next day, we had reservations to see Michelangelo's David, and I gave Mike a brief history of it. We then took him to Michelangelo's house. He was getting the benefit of our experience and knowledge and was realizing the importance of his heritage. That night, we took him to Ottorino, and we got the royal greeting by Giorgio, and as had become the norm, the plate of Fiore di zucca arrived, and Mike was overwhelmed. "Dad, we are eating flowers?"

The next morning, we left for Milano, but not before stopping for focaccia to eat on the train.

Once again, the usual stay at the Gallia was like coming home. We did not unpack. We jumped in a taxi and went to see *The Last Supper*, and I explained to Mike the history about both the treasures dating to the sixteenth century.

From there, we walked to the duomo and went in. Once again, Mike continued his amazement at the ability of the Italians to preserve these magnificent buildings and the art.

We dropped into the Galleria, and after seeing it, we walked to via Monte Napoleone, to another of our fine restaurants, Il Salumaio, and had great homemade ravioli, with the most incredible marinara sauce ever. We headed back to the hotel and rested until time for dinner. We had a seven-thirty reservation at Antica Trattoria della Pesa.

We took an early train to Venice the next morning, then a water taxi to Hotel Baglioni and went to lunch at Osteria di Fiore. The restaurant was jammed, and we waited thirty minutes to get a table and finally sat down to eat at two-thirty. Another lesson: the Italians, for the most part, stop everything at one o'clock across the country to eat and take time to relax, usually for two hours. Just about everything closes. Most businesses, factories, even the pharmacies! We had arrived at one-thirty. This was not a typical restaurant. The local businesspeople were dining, hence the wait.

We took a long walk after lunch, starting in St. Mark's Square, then crossed the Rialto Bridge, and finished the afternoon at the Guggenheim Museum.

We had dinner reservations at Harry's American bar and sat at the bar and had their famous Bellinis (freshly squeezed peach juice and Prosecco and a secret ingredient), and as is the norm, we waited for thirty minutes past our reserved seating time and ended up having the second Bellini. They were twelve dollars at the time, and we had another when we finally sat. As always, the food was the best. We have never had a bad meal there. We all ordered Risotto Milanese.

The following day, we took Mike to Murano and shared another lesson: take the water bus as opposed to the expensive water taxis. We then went to a typical glass blowing exhibition, and Mike bought an exquisite glass blown fish.

That night, we had our final dinner at Antico Martini, and afterward, we walked to St. Mark's piazza for an espresso.

The weather was delightful, and Mike expressed his gratitude. "Laurie and Dad, this has been the trip of my lifetime. I will be eternally grateful to you for all the planning you did, and I will never forget it. I had no idea what a great country this is, the people, the sites, the food, the lifestyle, but you guys really made the trip an experience!"

The next morning, we took the train back to Milano and flew to Chicago, confident that we were embarking on a prosperous future.

Laurie and I went to Las Vegas for the spa trade show. I watched her greet customers and saw how well she presented the new lines. It was a jam-packed show. I had no idea how many spas were in the country. Our sandal was ideal for the spas because of the hygienic problem with customers walking around barefoot. We convinced the owners that the unique Sensi drainage system would be ideal for their customers, particularly with the nonslip bottom and for usage in the showers. This was a good selling point because people would walk around after a massage with oil on their feet, and the floors were slippery.

The spas would have to carry a range of sizes as loaners for clients. The sandal was machine washable. This was a perfect introduction, as the spa client who enjoyed use would end up buying a pair.

In August, Doug Otto allowed us to show in the Deckers booth at the shoe show in Vegas. Laurie, Mike, and I did that show. We had quite a few appointments, thanks to the Deckers reps, and we came back with a stack of orders. The success continued with booking orders for spring, but we struggled through the fall when sales with the surf shops and shoe stores slowed. The spa business really helped pay the bills.

One of our shoe reps told us about a guy named Bob Simone, a freelance designer from Reebok's product development department who knew a lot about sneakers. We met with him and talked about possibly developing a Sensi sneaker, but we decided to table it until 1995. Bob was a good contact. He was quite involved in a project for himself and told us about a woman in Beverly Hills who was a good freelance sneaker designer. I kept her name in my book. We ended the year in the black and had made great progress.

In January 1995, Stephen Norris, our young spa rep in Phoenix, was cold calling on stores. He went into a sporting goods store and gave his best pitch to the manager, who responded, "I love your sandal, and I know we can sell it. We have nothing in the store like it. The problem is we are part of a thirty-six-store chain and the buying is done in Houston." He gave Stephen the buyer's name and contact information.

Unfortunately, this was Don Campbell's territory, and his son covered Houston. We protected territories to avoid conflicts between sales reps.

The fact remains that Don was not doing business with the store, and his son had never called on the buyer with Sensi. I gave Stephen the green light to contact the buyer. He did and flew to Houston the next week and came home with an order for 20,000 pairs of men's and women's sandals, totaling $220,000! I worked it out with Don, who chastised his son for not calling on the store.

There was no great secret to this success. In fact, it was quite simple. It was all a matter of our passion for the brand. We injected that passion into the veins of all of our employees and associates. And we treated them like family.

We made Lorenzo Sensi happy. We imported over 200,000 pairs for the year!

Painting of Santorini, Greece

CHAPTER 5

Ancona 1995

May 1995

In February, Laurie and I attended the Western shoe show in Las Vegas. Our reps from the west coast had many appointments, and business was good. Many of the old Sensi customers came to see us. We heard the same remarks, thanking us for taking back the license and carrying inventory for reorders. This was heartwarming news. But there still was the never-ending concern about the slowdown in the fall. I continued to stress to Laurie and Mike that we needed a product that we could market all year.

Laurie and I departed for Rome to once again to research sandal ideas of the Italian shoe designers. We did our usual routine of walking Via Condotti and the stores in the surrounding streets. We concluded the late morning shopping with our return to the Trevi Fountain, the Piazza dei Pantheon.

From the Piazza Navona, we walked to Campo de Fiore and had pizza at a bakery called Forno Campo de Fiore. We sat outside on a bench to enjoy it, happy as if we were in one of Italy's fine ristorante. Part of this had to do with the day. Once again, we were blessed. The weather was magnificent, not a cloud in the sky. The best part was watching the people. This was a neighborhood. People were shopping the open farmer's market to buy food for that afternoon's family lunch or dinner. This was the Italian way; they want everything fresh. That included bread from the bakery and vegetables and fruit from the open market. The Italians would never settle for produce picked green and sent to the market to hopefully ripen, as in the United States. They want it ripened on the plant. They shop almost daily for their ingredients. So sitting and eating our pizza, we were sharing the culture of Italians to put only the best in their stomachs.

That night, we tried another ristorante I had read about in *Vanity Fair* magazine, Caminetto. It was twenty minutes by taxi from the Piazza di Spagna, located in the Parioli district of the city. This was to our liking because it is where the locals ate, all speaking Italian, no tourists. We both ordered Risotto Milanese. The dish was resplendent with at least ten dollars worth of saffron. It was cooked to perfection.

Laurie asked me if I thought I could make risotto like it. I said, "Sure. Here's your deal. You buy the saffron and import the great Parmigiano that you get here (not what we get at home), and I will cook it for you."

She replied, "I have a better idea. You bring me back to this restaurant next time we are here, and I will buy dinner." We did that the next time we were in Rome.

The next morning, when we went to take the train to Assisi, we learned that most trains had been canceled. There was a strike by the engineers. Never a dull moment. I called our usual driver, but she was not available. She sent a driver friend who drove us to the Sensi factory. He remains our driver today.

At Sensi with Laura Bonci, we went to work and chose the new colors for the various styles and then broke for lunch. At lunch, Laura insisted we go to Ancona, her hometown, for a visit. I explained we had reservations in Firenze, and we tabled the decision until we returned to the office. She acted on our behalf and called our hotel, and they had no problem moving the reservation arrival two days later. She called her father to make hotel reservations for us for two nights. That night, we took the Sensi family and Laura to a great pizza restaurant for dinner and had a memorable evening. Here we were with a family we barely knew, sharing a meal in a tiny *trattoria*, discussing our family backgrounds. There was no haste for anything, and we did not get pushed to order. We ordered a bottle of wine and were served an appetizer, compliments of the chef, two incredible baby ravioli with a light tomato sauce. My curiosity rose again. Why is the pasta and pizza so much better in Italy? Years later we learned. It's the flour.

The Italian government does not allow the farmers to use pesticides on wheat as they do in the US. Also, the pasta shipped into the US must conform to various codes and ingredient specifications.

The next morning, Laura drove us to Ancona, which is in the Marche region on the east coast, and we were treated to a great family dinner with her mom, dad, and sister. The city dates back to the early Roman days and a major highlight is the Arch of Trajan, the Roman emperor, made out of marble. It is spectacular! It has beautiful white sand beaches along the Adriatic Sea. One of the most beautiful churches, San Cirico, sits atop the mountain overlooking the city. The next day, Saturday, she and her dad, Livio, took us on a tour of the area. We stopped for lunch in Fabriano and ate in a typical Marchese *trattoria*. The town is famous because it is where paper was first made from old rags. We had pasta with the purest marinara sauce we had ever tasted. Not a tomato seed nor a skin could be found. I made a comment of it, and Livio, who Laura had told us was a great cook, explained that to achieve those two things is a process. First you must use peeled canned tomatoes from San Marzano and fresh garlic and preferably a chopped sweet onion. After cooking only for thirty or forty minutes, put it through a food mill, which will catch any seeds. Also, do not cook the sauce with the garlic and onion. Remove both after deglazing the garlic and onion that have been sautéed with wine. Do not use cheap wine. Boil the pasta with salt to taste, and later when the raw pasta is nearly finished, drain it. Finish cooking it al dente in the pan with the sauce.

The next evening, Livio and Mrs. Bonci fixed pizza in their wood-fired oven and grated it with black truffles, another first. I had stopped with them on the way back from our sojourn that afternoon and bought two bottles of Tignanello red wine and surprised Livio when we returned to the house.

The next morning, Sunday, Laura and Laurie and I went to the beautiful town of Ascoli Piceno, which dates back to the early Roman days. We parked near the Piazza del Popolo, which was founded in the thirteenth century. It was full of local people from all over the area, including small towns outside of the city. Laura explained that friends would call each other early in the week to arrange to meet at a set time for mass and discuss what they were going to wear. It was like watching a fashion show. Men were in suits and ties, and the ladies were dressed like they were on a Paris runway displaying one of the great designers' latest collections.

We stopped for coffee in a typical caffe and had a cappuccino and an incredible brioche. I just shook my head after the first bite. "Why? Why can't we bake like this in the states? Here we are in the middle of nowhere savoring this pastry!" Laurie said, "First, the bakeries would never spend the money for the ingredients to bake it. The American people want cheap! McDonald's $0.99 burgers and baker's dozen doughnuts from Dunkin for $4.99."

As we were leaving, I noticed below the name of the caffe, Dal 1785 (founded 1785).

We went to the train station at noon with no reservations for Firenze, and Laura handed us a bag of mandarinos (baby tangerines) that were sweet as sugar and a box of Baci chocolate candies.

The train ride was three and a half hours, and after struggling with our luggage through four cars looking for seats, we finally opted to sit between cars on our bags. We began eating the mandarinos and later the chocolate to satisfy our hunger. Another lesson, have reservations for the trains.

Laurie was reading, and my mind started to drift, first at the relationship with the Sensi family. And now with the Boncis.

I was reminded when I first asked my former partner to join him on his June trip in 1984 to Assisi. He replied, "Mr. Sensi doesn't like Sicilians."

We finally arrived in Firenze and took a cab to the Loggiato hotel. We both were exhausted and hungry. The hotel had made dinner reservations when Laura had called for an early dinner at Ottorino. We both ate like we were scheduled for the electric chair the next day.

The trip was strictly to relax and stroll the city, eat, and drink some good wine for two days. The second night, while strolling back to the hotel after dinner, a very attractive young couple approached us and, in perfect Italian, asked, "*Mi scusi, signore, sa dove e la giarrettiera rossa.*" (Excuse me, sir. Do you know where the Red Garter is?)

I laughed and said, "What part of Brooklyn are you from?" They both laughed. They were college students studying in Firenze for a year. He was from New York, and she was from Santa Barbara. I knew the general area of the saloon and gave them directions, and after talking with them for a few minutes, we were back on our way to our hotel.

Laurie and I discussed what a great opportunity it was for those kids. We both traded stories of our lives at their age, me on the road for the Arrow company traveling parts of five states for $500 a month and Laurie working as a young architect for $18,000 a year.

We departed late the next morning for Milano after making the trip to the bakery for two large pieces of focaccia to eat on the way. Again, we had no agenda. It was for two nights. The plan was to window-shop the area around via Monte Napoleone and shop for sandal ideas and return once again to see the progress of the *Last Supper*.

The next day, we walked to Via Monte Napoleone and then to the Galleria and ended up with pizza from a takeout place across from the duomo. It was one of those beautiful days to play hooky, away from the grind and never-ending stress. It seemed there was no end to the pressure of getting the product development together.

We had dinner the second night at Aimo and Nadia, and the chef brought us a surprise when we finished dinner, a bag of his raw homemade spinach pasta and four tomatoes from his garden to take back to Chicago!

1995 was a good year, what with the spa business and back into Nordstrom with Sensi, our sales revenue reached $2,756,000, and we showed a nice profit.

My goal for 1996 was to get us back into Bloomingdales and some of the major department stores we had sold in the eighties. We had photos of advertisements by every major store in America, and I dug them out, and Laurie put them in a nice portfolio and designed an excellent cover for it. I made calls for appointments starting in New York, then down to Atlanta, and completed the first week in Miami with Burdines Department Store.

The following week, I went to Dallas and Houston. Next, the west coast and traveled from L.A. to San Francisco and finished the week in Seattle. We scored with every one of the major stores!

While 1995 was another good year, earnings from the business were not sufficient for us to live the lifestyle we enjoyed. Uppermost in my mind was to search for another business that was convenient to merge with the sales force, staff, and facility in Phoenix. Neither of us were taking a salary from the business. We did not need the income at this point.

We completed an eight-unit condominium investment project and made the decision not to get involved with another real estate development. The stress had gotten to us.

1996

We attended the Western shoe trade show in Las Vegas in February and had a very busy show. The attendance was way beyond previous shows. The best news was many of the major shoe chains visited our booth. We could smell that the Sensi resurrection was the right thing for us.

We returned to Chicago, and Laurie went to work on new sandal ideas and did color studies for the next line and sent them to the Sensi factory so they could get a head start on development for our next scheduled arrival.

In April, I had lunch with my attorney, Arnold Silvestri, and told him about our next trip to Italy. He asked, "Joe, have you been to Forte dei Marmi?"

I had never heard of it. "Where is it?"

"It is on the west coast, a short distance from Firenze." My former in-laws from Milano have a place there, and we used to meet them every year. It is a well-kept secret in Italy. You need to go. It will take any stress you are experiencing off your shoulders."

I researched it and found there was nothing of significance to do or see there. Also, I learned there was no train from Assisi. We would have to train to Firenze then by train to a nearby town and then by taxi. But we decided to give it a try, so I had my travel agent book us into one of the top hotels, the Hotel Byron. It was across the street from the beach.

In late May, we spent two days in Rome and then took the train to Assisi and worked on a new sandal design and finalized colors for the 1997 spring line.

When we arrived in Assisi, I asked Lorenzo about hiring a driver to take us to Forte dei Marmi, and he volunteered to take us.

We arrived in a heavy rainstorm and drove into a parking lot in front of a restaurant called Maito, and we treated the Sensis to a fresh seafood lunch. That fish was so fresh I would swear it was alive when they brought it to the table to show us before they baked it. The restaurant was right on the beach with an incredible view of the sea. We thanked them for driving us to our hotel, which was only a couple of minutes away. We hugged and said goodbye.

Within an hour, the rain stopped, and the bright sunshine dried everything. We took a map of the town and walked into the city center. World designers had their own shops, and the surprise was the mix of restaurants, outdoor caffes, flower shops, and galleries. It already cemented in our minds that this was to be a future haven for us.

Later on the walk back, we strolled the street along the Tyrrhenian Sea and discovered five restaurants on the sand along the way to the hotel.

When we returned, we had a conversation with the manager of the hotel and learned a little history of the area. The city sits below the Carrara mountains. He explained that the marble from them had been drawn since the early Roman days. We both asked how they got it down the mountain and then to Rome. He said, "They hauled it with oxen. Sometimes it would take months to arrive." He said, "Michelangelo's pure white marble also came from Carrara. Michelangelo was extremely meticulous and at times, would order pieces that were twenty feet tall! But after getting them down the mountain, if he found minor flaws, he would reject the piece. He wanted perfection."

We inquired about the restaurants, and he named his favorites. He liked Osteria del Mare, Maito, Tre Stelle, and Lorenzo, but he warned it was expensive.

Laurie asked, "What about pizza?" He said, "Without question, go to Bocconcino."

He made reservations for us at Tre Stelle that night, Osteria del Mare the next, and Lorenzo the last night.

He was right. Tre Stelle (Three Stars) was excellent. We dined outdoors, and the weather cooperated. It was a delightful evening. The food was superb, fresh fish and great roasted vegetables. We walked the area and found Bocconcino and decided to go there for lunch the next day. The shops spent a surprising amount of time and money on window displays of their merchandise. Contrary to the norm, they closed at one o'clock and reopened at four o'clock, and remained open until nine, so we were able to shop after dinner.

After breakfast the next morning, we took bicycles from the hotel, which we had noticed were a free option at all the hotels, and toured the surrounding area. We discovered beautiful villas everywhere we rode. Later, the manager told us some very distinguished wealthy Italians had summer homes, including Giorgio Armani.

We followed the manager's advice and headed to Bocconcino for pizza for lunch and were not disappointed. After stuffing ourselves, we walked the north part of town and found food shops and regular stores where the locals shopped. We made a note of a rotisserie that had great cheeses, prepared foods, and fresh homemade pastas and ravioli.

Laurie suggested, "Maybe tomorrow we should come here and do takeout and go eat in the park down the street." We did, and once again, we were delighted with our decision. The food was incredible, the weather was delightful, the park flowers scented the air, and we both had that warm Italian feeling of being home.

That night, we dined back at Maito, and the fish was roasted whole. We were served potatoes and vegetables from the same forno. We had a bottle of Cervaro with dinner and the cares of the world were not even a thought on our minds.

The next day, we walked the beach and saw the beautiful lounges and cabanas as far as one could see. The water was like bath water and clean. We walked to the downtown area and ended up by chance three blocks from Bocconcino. While waiting for pizza, I said, "Next time we come here, let's stay for a week. Laurie agreed. "You won't get an argument from me."

That night we went to Lorenzo, a five-star ristorante, and knew from the minute we walked in the door and saw all the beautiful people that we were in the high-rent district.

We were seated by Lorenzo himself. He looked like he just stepped out of a Fellini movie. Dressed as if Armani was his valet, he was charming.

A waiter approached with the wine list and menus, and I ordered a bottle of Livio Felluga Terre Alte white wine. The waiter was shocked. He had already qualified us, perhaps with the way we were dressed. He determined we were not part of the beautiful people.

Within minutes, we were served an appetizer, an incredible ravioli stuffed with lobster, and a light cream sauce. That prompted Laurie to say, "I know what I'm having for dinner, more of these."

We toasted each other and looked at the menu. Laurie said, "Joe, my menu has no prices."

I replied, "That's to entice you to order expensive items." The meal was the best of the entire trip, well worth the price. The best part was there were no tourists.

We headed to Milano for the final two days of the trip. We were told by the hotel manager there was no direct train. We had to go to Genoa and change trains, and he checked the computer for schedules. There was a train departing for Genoa at eleven, and we could easily make the connection at two-thirty for the three hours to Milano. He said, "You will easily be in Milano in time for dinner."

I suggested to Laurie, "Let's go to the rotisserie and have them make two panini to take on the train." When we got there, the lady behind the counter had just taken a veal roast out of the forno. She cut two nice pieces of focaccia and sliced that veal paper-thin and drizzled some of the natural gravy on it. All I could think of was the vegetables, carrots, potatoes, and onions that had been cooked with the roast. There was no way to include them, so it rested in my head for our return another day. We figured we'd eat them once we arrived in Genoa. They barely made it to the train station in Forte.

The trip was no problem. Both trains were older, but we found a private compartment in the car for Milano, and we both napped. We checked into the Gallia to the usual warm welcome. That night, we chose to dine at Hostaria Borromei. What a meal! We had risotto con Piselli fresco (risotto with fresh peas).

What had become the order of the day, our first stop the next day was to see the progress of *The Last Supper*. The lady was making significant headway and was ahead of her twenty-year plan. It seemed like she had completed half of the restoration.

We followed our usual pattern: walked to the Galleria and had an espresso, then to Monte Napoleone and had lunch in our courtyard ristorante.

That night, we dined at Celestino because Trattoria Della Pesa was closed, but we returned there our last night. We flew to Chicago the next day.

We had our sales meeting in August, and along with the sales force, we began selling the spring 1997 line.

We worked all the trade shows the rest of the year, and once again, revenue was up, as were profits. Our hard work and the passion we injected into the entire staff was paying off. But the never-ending fall and winter slowdown in sales was still there. I was determined to find something to offset the seasonal impact of the sandal.

Beach cabanas in Forte dei Marmi

CHAPTER 6

A Page Turns in the Imaginary Book

In January 1997, Laurie and I went to our home in Palm Springs for a well-earned rest. We were looking forward to relaxing, eating, sleeping, and sunning. I was reading the 3,000-year history of Sicily, yearning to learn about my homeland. My sister, Josie, and Joe were in Palm Springs and were completing their trip to my desert Shangri-La. I convinced them to stay a few extra days with us. She and Joe had been to Sicily twice, and we had discussions about family ties. The fact our mother had gone in 1959 for three months was the main topic of discussion.

I was enthralled with the history because of the book I was reading. Sicily was discovered and civilized by the Greeks, along with the Carthaginians 3,000 years before Christ was born. We ultimately decided to go together in September.

Later that month, I received a call from our sales rep in Florida, Scott Bechtold. He was the number one salesperson in the country and my protege, who thought of me like an uncle. He had originally gone to work for us in 1976 when he was twenty years old, packing jeans in the warehouse for five dollars an hour.

"Uncle Joe, why don't you see if you can get the license for Tommy Bahama for shoes? You know Bob Emfield, one of the owners. Their line is hot. It is in every store down here."

"Scott, you must be kidding. We don't know anything about making shoes. There are 150 shoe companies in this country. Why would they license us?"

Two weeks later, my son, Mike, was in the Florida Keys on a fishing trip, and he called.

"Dad, I was just in a store here, and it looks like a Tommy Bahama Store. At least seventy percent of the men's apparel is Tommy Bahama!"

"So, Mike, what do you want me to do?"

"Doesn't your friend own part of it?"

"Yes, so have you talked to Bechtold? Are you asking me to put an arm on Bob and get down on my knees and ask for the license for footwear?"

"That's exactly what I am suggesting."

"Okay, Mike." I had no intention of calling Bob.

In February, we were at the Magic apparel trade show in Las Vegas, the largest apparel trade fair in the world. It was international. Shoe and clothing manufacturers from all over the world were represented.

Another page turned in the large book up in the sky. Mike called and said there was a meeting with all the lead buyers from Nordstrom, and they wanted Sensi samples for their appointment and an audience at the show. They would not commit to a fixed time. "Dad, you have to be here." I agreed.

The page turned, and who is walking by? Bob Emfield and Lucio Dalla Gasperina, the head of Tommy Bahama merchandising and product development. Bob looked at me and greeted me, as always, with respect and introduced Lucio, and I asked in my terrible Italian, "Sei Italiano?" (Are you Italian?)

He responded in perfect Dante Italian, "I am. I was born in Firenze."

"Ah, my favorite city in the world!"

"Have you been there?" he asked.

"Yes. We make sandals in Assisi, and we visit Firenze every time we go to Italy."

"Joe, I thought you sold Sensi to the people at Ugg."

"We did, Bob. They paid me a lot of money for it, and it took them less than two years to screw it up! Are you guys thinking about doing any footwear?"

Bob answered, "We are thinking about doing a sneaker and a few sandals."

"We know a little about the sandal business, Bob, and we have a sneaker in the works too. Please throw my name in the hat once you have made a decision. You know we can produce products to your liking." I was focusing my attention on Lucio as well as Bob.

They briefly walked through our booth, and Bob showed Lucio the sandal.

Mike, Scott, and I could not believe what had just transpired.

Laurie and I went back to Palm Springs after the show. Within a week, the phone rang. It was Bob. He was in New York, and his partner, Tony Margolis, was on the phone. We talked for a few minutes about their thoughts regarding our product and the timeline to create and produce samples. The discussion advanced to a point beyond small talk quickly.

Margolis asked, "Would you want a license or a joint venture?" I immediately said, "I would prefer a fifty-fifty joint venture."

Tony said, "How much money would we need to start?"

I replied, "We have a warehouse and a well-trained staff. We do not need to buy any equipment. All we need is product and sales. Let's start with $250,000, $125K each."

Bob grasped the ball and asked, "How soon can you put some samples together?"

I said, "For one real nice sneaker and two sandals, we can have them ready for approval in sixty days."

Tony said, "Let's get Lucio on the phone."

I could see Lucio was not getting Tony's drift. Tony's thoughts were the expansion of the brand with licensees, getting huge profits from license fees with no investment or risk.

It was my turn. "Lucio, you don't know me. Would you be open to me flying to Seattle with our shoe designer? She is freelance and has quite a portfolio with top firms on her work. We can be there any day next week. All I need is an hour of your time to discuss our track record. I have been in the sandal business for thirteen years."

We set a date for the following Tuesday.

We had made contact with the shoe designer a year or so back. Her name was Sally McGee, and she had an office in Beverly Hills. I called her, and we agreed to meet at the Seattle airport.

We were picked up by our Seattle rep Bruce Condiotty, who knew Lucio, and went to the Tommy Bahama office. Sally showed her portfolio first, and then I showed the book Laurie had designed with thirteen years of ads and publicity about Sensi.

Luccio asked, "Who does your public relations?"

I told him about Janet Orsi, who handled it for us and Massimo, the hottest young men's line in the country. There was no doubt we convinced him we had the credentials to make this work. He invited us to lunch at a very nice Italian restaurant. We spent more time at lunch than we had at the office. I made it a point to avoid business, restrained from continuing the discussion at the office. I am a firm believer of that philosophy. Most people spend eight to ten hours a day at their job. The last thing they want to do is continue to be besieged at mealtime with more business. Leave business back at the office. I directed the whole discussion on my love for Italy and got Lucio to discuss his favorite places.

A week after my return to Chicago, Margolis called and wanted Janet Orsi's phone number. We spent over an hour on the phone discussing the joint venture, and he said he would have their corporate lawyer put together a rough draft of the agreement and asked for our lawyer's name and number. We decided to call the new venture "Paradise Shoe Company."

I said, "Tony, I know how to read. I do not need an attorney. Give him my number, and here is my fax number. Have him fax the document to me, and let's get the ball rolling. You want salesman's samples ready by July. We have less than three months."

A week later, I received the contract for the venture and license agreement calling for a six percent royalty fee on total annual sales. I signed it and sent it back to the attorney.

I made immediate plans to go to Italy with Laurie, specifically Rome, Firenze, and Milano, to shop for footwear ideas and confirm our color direction.

We flew to Rome for two nights and searched the key footwear stores to see what the Italian designers had in the stores for casual footwear that fit the Tommy Bahama image. The next day, we took the early train to Firenze with the same premise. We stayed only one night but took really good display window photos for ideas.

Next was Milano for two nights. We spent a good deal of time both days in and around Via Monte Napoleone. We bought some nice leather sandals, both men's and women's. We took time to visit and witness the progress of *The Last Supper*. No trip to Milan could be complete without dinner at Antica Trattoria della Pesa.

The next morning, we took the early morning flight back to Chicago.

In mid-May, we flew to L.A. again to meet with Sally and two people from a firm in San Francisco. They had contacts with a company in Taiwan that had connections with a shoe factory in China. We came to an agreement to make the first samples of a sneaker and two sandals. The sneaker design was modified for women.

In early June, we received the first samples, and we approved them with minor changes and sent the label designs we had received back to the factory. Ten days later, we received the revised samples with the labels and ordered sales samples.

In mid-July, we flew to Seattle for the Tommy Bahama sales meeting, and Laurie presented the three shoes to the three owners of the firm and the sales force. We got a green light to proceed, with the understanding that their sales force would control distribution first to their apparel stores. Our sales group could sell the shoe stores in each town, only if the existing clothing store refused to buy the shoes. Our sales reps hands were tied, but my goal was to bring both sales groups together. I put a plan into effect so that they could work hand and hand in each territory. I did not want our reps to step on any toes. We needed to avoid controversy. The reps got together and reviewed the Tommy accounts in each city, and our salepeople had a pretty good idea of who they could sell.

Those clothing stores that did not sell shoes opened the door for our reps to pursue the shoe stores in each city.

In September, we flew to Rome and met my sister, Josie, and Joe Mocca, had a sandwich at the airport, and later boarded a plane for Sicily. We flew to Catania, rented a car, and drove to Taormina, and checked into the Hotel Villa Carlotta. I had finished reading the 3,000-year history of Sicily and shared some of the fascinating facts, including the raping of the island by invaders from several countries. We had dinner reservations for all three nights that I had asked the hotel to make. We walked the entire town in those three days and marveled at the sites. The Teatro Antico (old Greek theatre) looked like it was built six months ago. It could house 40,000 people. It truly was amazing. We walked the Corso Umberto and loved the shops and the people. The weather was perfect. We stopped for coffee at a quaint caffe and rested.

I thought back about my mom and a trip we had taken to the wine country north of San Francisco and her strong suggestion to visit Sicily. She was ecstatic about the warm welcome she had from both her side and my father's side of the family. She knew how much I loved fresh figs, and she said, "Go in early September. The figs grow wild along the streets and roads!"

I said to Laurie, "Why have we waited so long to come here?"

We concluded our walk and visited the beautiful gardens in the park, and that night, we had dinner at La Cucina di Riccabona, simple home-cooked Sicilian food. We had great artichokes. The leaves were spread open and stuffed with grated cheese and garlic and drizzled with olive oil and baked. Parmigiana, sliced thin eggplant, lightly fried in olive oil, layered in casseroles with tomato sauce, and grated parmigiano and baked.

The pasta was called Pasta Norma. It was mixed with fresh tomatoes, basil, grilled chunks of eggplant, garlic, topped with ricotta and pecorino grated cheese. We were shocked. The prices were half that of Italy.

Our dining experiences the last two nights were the same. Nothing fancy but great food consisting of excellent Sicilian wines, and we enjoyed the relaxed culture of the Sicilian people.

We drove to Casteltermini, the birthplace of my parents, the next morning, and Josie knew exactly the small house where my mother was born. It was not much of a building, but Josie said it had been in the family for four generations. We could not enter because it no longer belonged to the family. We then went to visit a cousin and her husband. They were expecting us. Their home was very contemporary and well-furnished. Her name was Maria Insalaco, and she and her husband had a greenhouse, and they grew all types of tomatoes. They had enough food prepared to feed a battalion. They were from my mother's side of the family. There was fried fish amongst all kinds of fresh vegetables. Laurie stuck with the vegetables and begged off the fish. She was smarter than me, for later that evening, I got sick from the fish. A cousin named Luigi Reina had driven from Palermo to visit us. We spent the entire afternoon with them, and I got the message my mom had tried to send me about our family. I was home.

Later, we departed around six-thirty for Agrigento to continue to tour the country. Josie and Joe had elected to spend the next six days in Casteltermini. They were going to take a train and meet us toward the end of the trip in Cefalu for a couple of days.

When we arrived in Agrigento, I was ill, too sick to eat, we opted to dine in the hotel restaurant. Laurie had a light dinner, and we retired. The next morning, I felt better, and at ten, we met a guide for a tour of a Greek temple that dated four hundred years BC! He explained in detail the history behind it. It is called the Temple of Concordia, the Roman goddess. In the sixth century, it was converted to a Catholic church by the head of the diocese of Agrigento. Some restoration was performed in the eighteenth century, but the overall condition was unbelievable.

According to the history of Sicily I read, the Greeks and the Cartaginians founded the Island 800 years before Christ was born.

Rome conquered the Island about 250 BC. They needed to grow wheat all year long to make bread to feed their armies. Through the years, Spain, Austria, the French, the Moors as well as Naples ruled and raped it. In 1861, General Garibaldi of the Italian army rescued it from control of Naples and made it part of the unification of Italy.

And then the Mafia in the nineteenth century emerged and controlled it for over a century, leaving the economy decimated. The young people left in droves over the years because there were no jobs, especially in small towns.

Laurie and I had plans to visit the Ancient Greek temples in Segesta and in Selinunte, and our amazement continued, and two days later, we arrived in Palermo. We hooked up with my cousin on the Reina side, who visited with us in Casteltermini, and received a royal welcome. Palermo is a beautiful city full of great things to see and do. We did not plan enough time there, but we vowed to return.

Later, we drove to Cefalu and checked into our hotel, then walked around the city. The weather continued to favor us. It was the climax of another beautiful day. That night, we had dinner at a great ristorante, La Brace. I read about it in *Travel and Leisure.*

The next morning, we picked up Josie and Joe at the train station and had lunch at Teresa, a tiny little place that served only twelve people. It was out of this world. We had stumbled on it, and the smells were like being in Josie's basement on any given holiday. Cefalu is a beautiful seaside village on the north side of Sicily and well worth a visit.

The next day, we drove to Catania, turned in the rental car, flew to Rome, and caught a flight to Chicago the next morning.

For spring of 1998, we shipped one hundred percent of what we purchased in Tommy Bahama and showed a nice profit. This was largely due to little overhead expense. Neither Laurie, Mike, or I took a salary in 1997 or 1998. Needless to say, the Tommy partners were pleasantly surprised.

Laurie and I flew to Rome and did our usual routine, spending only two nights, and then took the train to Firenze. We had arranged to meet Riccardo Betticinni, an agent who had been recommended. He spoke enough English that there was no language barrier. We went to three men's and one ladies shoe factory. Once again, Laurie's curiosity surfaced, and she spent a great deal of time in the factories watching the step-by-step process of making a pair of shoes.

We did not see anything that fit the Tommy Bahama lifestyle in the collections of those factories.

We did our window shopping in Firenze the next day and took many photos, and we purchased a few pairs of shoes that had interesting ideas we could share with Sally.

After two days, we moved on to Milano, shopped Via Monte Napoleone, paid our visit to the *Last Supper*, and after two nights, flew back to Chicago with additional ideas for Sally McGee.

She flew to Chicago for two days, and we shared our thoughts on direction for the next line release for spring 1999. We agreed to meet in March to see her sketches and design ideas for both men and women.

In February, we attended the Magic show in Las Vegas and walked the show. We spent a great deal of time in the international section and met two people in the Spain section from a company called Cidon. They displayed some very nice ladies' sandals and casual loafers, and we struck a deal on prices and asked them to make prototypes with the Tommy Bahama label for us.

Our sales were excellent thanks to the Tommy Bahama sales reps bringing their buyers to our section of the show booth.

We flew to L.A. mid-March and found Sally totally unprepared. She had hurriedly put a few sketches of warmed up ideas of the current line together and admitted she was too busy on projects she was doing for other clients. I elected to end the relationship.

We flew back to Chicago and started searching for design help.

Time was of the essence because we had three months to get something together for the spring 1999 line release.

Through friends at the Florsheim shoe company, I made contact with a senior vice president of the largest chain of retail shoe stores in the world. His wife designed shoes for one of Florsheim's designer licensees. We arranged for a meeting at our home. Their names were Scott and Loretta Sanders. We checked out her portfolio and made a quick decision to go to Italy with them. She promised to do some sketches to take with us. They explained they had three factories in Verona that had great collections we could select from and adapt them for our brand. The option also existed to make minor changes.

We had no choice. Our backs were to the wall. We left the first week of April and flew to Milan. Scott had a one-day meeting in Venice, and we joined them. It had been a while since we had been there. Scott made hotel arrangements, and we checked into the hotel Europa, normally too expensive for us.

Laurie and I had the next day to ourselves. As I was unpacking, Laurie picked up the hotel magazine, which listed the month's events and said, "Joe, our favorite museum Palazzo Grassi is featuring all the drawings and sketches of Leonardo da Vinci's *Last Supper*. Let's do it tomorrow." We went to lunch at Trattoria alla Rivetta and walked around St. Marks, and we ended up back at the hotel exhausted because of the time difference.

That night, we had reservations at Harry's American Bar at eight o'clock and were right on time, but as is always the case, we were told it would be a few minutes for our table. The maitre'd suggested we go to the bar.

We had Bellinis, and at 8:20, I said to the bartender, "*Signore la nostra prenotazione e per otto.*" (Sir, our reservation was for eight.) He smiled, turned around, and reached for the long arm of the clock on the wall behind him and moved it to 7:45. We ordered another Bellini.

We finally were seated and ordered another Bellini. This is their plan. They know once you get started on them, it is not easy to stop, but the food was worth the wait. We started with scampi and then risotto con asparagi for our secondo. The ambiance and service coupled with the food make it, in my book, one of the all-time great restaurants in all of Italy.

The next morning, we walked to Museo Grassi. It was once a palazzo originally owned by the Grassi family and dates back to the seventeenth century. It was primarily used as a villa and later fell into disrepair. The Angneli family (Fiat auto company) bought it around 1983 and did extensive renovation and planned to use it for events and theatre.

Later, a wealthy Frenchman purchased it and did more renovation before turning it into a museum.

All three floors of this incredible facility were dedicated to Leonardo's three-year study, preparing for painting the *Last Supper*.

All of his well-preserved sketches were on display, well protected from touch, and the rooms were thermostatically controlled.

I commented to Laurie as we walked, "Only in this country can we be walking amongst this incredible collection of priceless art that dates back to the sixteenth century." It showed da Vinci's precise talent, sketches of the apostle's hands, neck, arms, feet, and legs under the table, including their sandals. Their faces were drawn with such detail that it seemed as if any given moment they would begin speaking! Read *Leonardo da Vinci* by Walter Isaacson.

Leonardo had spent years cutting up cadavers in order to study and learn every part of human anatomy and had voluminous drawings to help with the sketches we were seeing.

We spent the entire morning there and left when the Museo closed at one o'clock.

We went to a tiny *osteria* for lunch and had a plate of pasta and a carafe of vino. The rest of the afternoon was spent walking the city. We met Loretta and Scott for dinner at Da Forni.

We agreed to meet for breakfast the next morning and to head for Verona.

Laurie has a talent for scoping out people, and she said, "Joe, something is bothering me about these people. I don't know what it is. I hope I am wrong. Why did they bring us here? We could have met them in Verona." I said, "You worry too much. We are running out of time. Let's see what happens in Verona. They have a lot of experience, and right now we need them."

CHAPTER 7

Verona

The four of us took the train to Verona then a taxi to the Mariton shoe factory, where we met the owners, and reviewed their current men's collection. It was massive. We found two loafers that fit the Tommy Bahama lifestyle, and were impressed with both the quality and the prices. We were told the shoes were cut and sewn in Romania, and finished in their factories in Verona. We ordered prototypes with the Tommy Bahama label. Afterward, we toured the factory and then we were off to a ladies shoe factory. It was primarily a dress shoe, expensive factory that didn't fit the Tommy casual apparel customer. Scott said, "I think you'll like the next firm, Rosetta. They design and make casual footwear, everything is made right here in Verona."

We arrived right in time to go to lunch. The factory was run by second-generation children, We met the owner Giorgio San Fillippo, Rudy Ferrara the designer, and Lidia Baldo, Rudy's assistant, she was the only one who spoke English. We went to a small *Osteria* for lunch which gave us time to tell the Tommy Bahama story, and the type of product for which we were searching.

When we returned to the factory, we were impressed with their current collection and selected a small group of samples. Loretta and Laurie went to work modifying them and made a few color selections for prototypes. We were informed it would only take a couple of weeks for them to get the samples to us. Again we were impressed with the factory, and the people, especially Lidia Baldo. She was a warm, attractive young woman.

That night, we had dinner in the city center at Al Pompiere, a very fine ristorante near our hotel, the Victoria. After dinner, we strolled the area and were astounded at the beauty of this well kept secret. Anyone going to Venice either by train, bus, or automobile must pass Verona, and usually they pass. The main piazza, Piazza della Erbe, dates back to early Rome. It doesn't require much imagination to realize what life was like in the Roman days. The shops and ristoranti all had extensive palazzos above them. We learned that the wealthy Romans spent summers there because it is north and much cooler. I commented, "It must have been incredible in the early days for wealthy Romans to come here and stay in their homes for the summer with their families. I'm sure they had servants to do everything for them. To shop for food, cook for them, and service all their needs." Laurie said, "From what I have read, they were the rich that had it all, including slaves, while the "Plebes" worked and paid the taxes to support Roman wars.

Later, we strolled to an area Scott suggested called Piazza Bar. There was an exact duplicate of the Colosseum, in much better condition than the one in Rome. It was built in the first century and appears like it was built a year ago. It was originally used as a Roman amphitheater. Today, it's a venue for concerts and other events. We strolled the shopping area near the colosseum, and were amazed.

The streets were marble, all very narrow, few cars were allowed; the marble was weathered from years of wear, but typical of the way the Italians do things. No one knows how long ago that marble had been laid, it would last lifetimes, and that was by design. The next morning we departed for Firenze. We asked Loretta to go to Spain to work with the people at Cidon whom we met at the previous show in Las Vegas. We sent a fax to Mariano Cidon to expect her. She and Scott went their separate ways.

Laurie and I checked into the beautiful Ferragamo-owned Hotel Lungarno. We unpacked and strolled across the Ponte Vecchio to the Piazza Signoria and to Cantinetta dei Verrazzano for our focaccia fix. It was like coming home. We had gotten to know the city by now and knew our way around. We could not have ordered better weather; it was a delightful day, and as always, I had trouble believing we were walking in this spectacular city; it was surreal. Afterward, we had a gelato and walked without care or agenda. I said, "I was pleased about the trip with the Sanders and especially with the Rosetta factory. It will be a major resource for making women's shoes." Laurie nodded, "I like the fact that they have Lidia and Rudy and the shoes are made there, so they can control the entire process."

We had dinner that night at Cantinetta Antinori for the first time. Antinori is one of the largest wineries in Italy and makes some of our favorite wines. I asked the waiter his favorite thing on the menu. He suggested the Ravioli for our pasta dish." And the "Vitello Cotoletta" (veal cutlet), for "il secondo" (second dish). We ordered a bottle of Cevaro, our favorite white wine.

The next morning, we took the train to Milano, and stayed at the Gallia, and did the usual. We window shopped Via Monte Napoleone, and all the shoe stores in and around it. Later we walked to see the continued restoration of the *The Last Supper*. We marveled at the patience of the lady artist doing the restoration. I said, "Can you imagine the responsibility of her daily touching this trusted treasure, and how careful she has to be." Laurie responded,"We are so fortunate to be able to come here and watch a bit of history in the making."

That night, we had dinner at a new restaurant I had read about, Coco Lazzoni. Once again, I took a card, and later when we returned to Chicago, I put the name in my book, we agreed we must return, the food was outstanding. I commented to Laurie, "It is amazing to me how different the cuisine is between and north and the south. In the south, it is pasta with red sauce, and in the north, it is risotto.

And also in the north a lot of food with cream sauces, I am sure it was influenced by the French when they controlled northern Italy.

Shortly after returning to the States, I hit the road to work with the sales reps, starting in New York and down to Florida, and on to a trade show in Dallas. I spent the weekend working with both the Tommy sales team, and our reps, Michele and Larry Brenner, two old friends from Chicago. We were booking shoes for fall 1998 and getting good reactions to the small line we had put together as well as reorders on Sensi. I flew to John Wayne airport after the show on Monday and rented a car and drove to Laguna Beach and checked into the Surf and Sand hotel. The next morning, Bob Ritz, the Tommy regional sales rep, and I drove to Newport Beach to call on Gary's, the finest men's store in Southern California. We had a meeting with Dick Braeger, the owner, who had been one of the owners of Cole Hahn shoe company. Bob told me, "This guy has forgotten more about the shoe business than you will ever learn, so do not do anything to try to impress him. He has heard it all."

We met Dick. He was somewhat of a legend in the shoe business. I must admit, I was a little intimidated before we walked into his office. I walked softly in my presentation. He was a huge Tommy Bahama apparel account and had a beach and surf type store with a Hawaiian flavor across from Gary's. It might as well have been a Tommy Bahama store. Over seventy-five percent of the apparel was Tommy. What a great store. My immediate thought was how perfect it was for Sensi. I made a mental note to get with Dick and our Sensi rep at a later date. More importantly, to start tying in the whole Tommy Bahama account base with Sensi. Next, I flew to Seattle. Our salesperson Bruce Condiotty drove us to meet with the Nordstrom people. Nordstrom was the largest Tommy Bahama account in the country. We met with Blake Nordstrom, the CEO. I had not seen him in years, but he remembered me. He gave me a test order for Sensi in 1984 and rattled off my Sensi sales pitch about the versatility of the sandal. We laughed. We discussed the fact that we were producing footwear with the Tommy Bahama label and explained that some of his shoe buyers had not purchased the line. We explained they didn't really know how important the brand was to the store. At the time, every store had its own buyer for both men's and ladies' shoes. He promised he would help get the word out.

In June, I called Bob Emfield and told him, "Belts go with shoes, and we should be doing casual belts that go with Tommy Bahama apparel. I had studied the belts at Dick Braeger's stores and at Nordstrom and found dress belts. No one was showing casual belts." Bob was right on it and agreed. "Do some belts, and get back to me."

At the previous shoe show in Las Vegas, Bruce Condiotty, our Seattle rep, took me into a show booth for Mezlan, a very fine shoe company from Spain. He introduced me to Jeff Thornton, the sales rep for California. Mezlan was owned by Antonio Sanchez. I called Jeff, got Antonio's phone number, and placed a call. I introduced myself and told him we were in a joint venture with Tommy Bahama, and he said he had never heard of the brand. I was shocked. I asked, "Would you be willing to make some belts for us? We do not want dress belts. We want casual belts." He was hesitant. I could see that and stopped trying to sell him on the idea on the phone.

"Antonio, let me and my wife fly out to California and come to your office. I have a proposition for you." He agreed, and we set a date for the following week. The next week, we flew to John Wayne airport and drove to his office. We showed him our line sheets and gave him ideas on what we felt he needed to design a few belts. We spent the day working on the design of twelve belts. Antonio told us we would have prototype samples in three weeks. He said, "I am leaving for Spain next week and will put this top priority at the factory." I replied, "Antonio, at some point, we want to go to the factory and meet the people." We are starting to make ladies shoes with a factory there, and we need to visit them." He said, "Joe, I may be able to help you with your production on both men's and ladies' shoes."

"How much volume do you think you can do in belts?" I explained the process that we had to get approval of the belts by Tommy Bahama first, but I assured him we could do $1,000,000 in sales the first year, which was $450,000 at cost from the factory.

He said, "That's a lot of belts." He agreed to work on a straight ten percent commission on the cost of the belt. The three of us had dinner that night, and I told Laurie afterward, "This is going to be a major contact for us." Three weeks later, we received the belt samples from Spain. I called Bob Emfield, and he flew to Chicago to see them. We were operating out of a small office in a building I owned, and I was embarrassed to bring him there, so I brought him to our house to look at the belts. He liked them and called Tony and Lucio and said, "I am with Joe Reina. We are in the belt business." Bob explained, "To get approval, we need to show these samples to my partners before ordering final salesman samples." We had a sales meeting in July and agreed to show them at the meeting. I could not have been happier. What a call meeting Antonio. We did not know the first thing about making a belt, nor did we know where to locate a quality belt factory. Antonio had explained he was buying leather and buckles in Italy to make his belts. He said, "It would behoove us to do the same to ensure the quality we wanted for the Tommy belts but told us they would be more expensive than using Spanish materials."

At the meeting, I presented the belts to the group, and one by one, all but two were rejected. Needless to say, we were disappointed, but we did not argue. The last thing I wanted was to get into a disagreement with the powers to be. We were in Seattle, and we still had to show the spring 1999 shoe line. After our presentation, I called Antonio and gave him the news. He said, "Can you fly to Southern California after your meeting? We can go back and work on some new styles and use the comments from your meeting to make improvements." One of those suggestions was regarding the buckles. They wanted solid brass, expensive buckles. In addition, they wanted more detail on the belts themselves. Some were rejected because they were too plain. We flew to California the next day, disappointed but not discouraged. I told Laurie, "I am convinced Antonio can deliver nice, high-quality belts. It is no different than what we are experiencing in footwear. We need to continue the learning process, finding the right factories and improving design and quality. It will take time." We sat with Antonio for the next day and a half, starting from the design of the two belts they had approved and came up with ten new designs. Once again, Antonio promised prototypes in three weeks. In early August, Laurie and I flew to Milano, did the usual window shopping at the Monte Napoleone stores. We checked on the progress of *The Last Supper*. We witnessed the artist in her meticulous, tedious renovation of this beautiful treasure.

That night, dinner was at our favorite ristorante, Antica Trattoria della Pesa. The next day, we took a taxi to the Galleria. We marveled at the crowd. It was one of those beautiful days. The sun was gleaming down the front of the duomo. Throngs of people were enjoying themselves, walking with their gelato or sitting on a bench with a slice of pizza. Inside the Galleria, there was not a seat to be found at any of the ristoranti or caffes. I said to Laurie, "Let's walk to via Monte Napoleone to see what is going on there." We did and found the same excitement. It was Saturday in Milano. The streets were full of tourists and classy Italians enjoying the sites, scenes, and food in this robust exciting city. Milano had been described to me by my former partner in the sandal business as a large industrial city. He said, "Don't waste your time going there. It is a crowded big city, not much to see or do." We stopped for a gelato and continued to stroll the streets in and around via Monte Napoleone and finally decided to head back to the hotel. We took the train Sunday for Verona and Lidia Baldo from Rosetta took us to the hotel Victoria. She suggested we go to Lago di Garda for lunch.

We did not unpack. We had cappuccino at the hotel and drove to Castelnuovo, a small town, with an old castle and a stream and waterfall running through it. We treated Lidia to lunch at a very nice *osteria*. I remarked to Lidia about the food, the vegetables, and the pasta. I said, "It is hard to understand. We never get so much as a mediocre meal, even in small places like this." She replied, "We Italians are spoiled. We are used to eating good food at home, and we will not stand for fast food. The people in the ristorante are aware of this. I have been to the United States many times, and it seems like the people in the restaurants hurry to seat you and rush to get your order. They rush you to eat and want you to leave so that they can get the next party to your table. Here, usually, when we sit down, we understand everything is cooked to order. We know it takes time, so they aren't expecting anyone else for our table." We walked around the town, and once again, the weather was delightful. Lidia asked if we wanted an espresso. She said she would like to take us to another town along the lake for it, or we could sit and have it here. We opted for the next town.

We drove to Desenzano and marveled at this latest treasure. It seemed there was no end to the incredible surprises. Desenzano was entirely different from the first town. Well-preserved, older, and just as quaint and romantic. We walked around and finally stopped at a small caffe with seating outside along the lake. I mentioned that in both towns, there were no English-speaking tourists. Lidia said, "That is because it is difficult to get here. Most people coming to this part of Italy from the United States go to Venice. Those that sometimes stop for one day to visit Verona do not have the time to come to the lake." We departed, and she drove us to our hotel and asked if we would like to go for pizza that night to one of her favorite places. I said, "Laurie has never met a pizza she didn't love," and we agreed to meet back at the hotel lobby at seven-thirty to walk to the ristorante. After she left, my instinct about people kicked in, and I said to Laurie, "Lidia is going to become a major contact and friend for a long time." She agreed. The ristorante was Vicolo Regina d'Ungheria, and the pizza was great, never a disappointment, and only locals were dining. The only language spoken was Italian. You will not find it on the internet by TripAdvisor. That's the beauty of being with a local person.

On Monday morning, Lidia picked us up and took us to the factory. Rudy and Lidia presented their samples for the next line. From time to time, Georgio came in to check on us. We were both impressed at how well-prepared they were. They had samples for us that were labeled Tommy Bahama. No question, they had a passion for the brand. We broke for lunch and went to a small town in the hills above Verona called Belvedere. Lidia said the ristorante only served fresh homemade pastas. Their specialty was tortellini with various sauces. Six ladies arrive at five o'clock every morning to make them. The dough is so light and thin you can almost see through it. Georgio ordered a bottle of white wine and then, in Italian, ordered for the table. I didn't understand a word he said and whispered to Lidia, "Did he just order for us?" She confirmed. We toasted each other, and soon we were served *tortellini in brodo* (tortellini in broth). There was silence. It was so good. No one was speaking. Next was the second course. The tortellini was stuffed with spinach and Parmigiano arrived with a Bolognese sauce. After the first course, I could not believe it could be topped, but it was. And for the finale, tortellini stuffed with veal with a marinara sauce that rivaled what we had with Livio Bonci. Not a seed or skin from the tomatoes in the sauce. I commented, "Lidia, I now understand what you meant about the dough being so thin. They were very light. I can't believe we just consumed three plates of tortellini, and I am not stuffed."

Laurie said, "I could go for another course." Georgio took her seriously and was ready to order it, but I stopped him. After an espresso, we went back to work. We finished, and Lidia took us back to the hotel. Giorgio had insisted we have dinner, and I accepted on the condition I get the check. We went to Nuovo Marconi and were seated immediately. Giorgio told the server to be sure he would get the check, and I understood what he said. I jumped right at both of them and told the waiter on no uncertain terms, *"Il conto e per mi."* He got the message. He received the Reina look. Georgio ordered a bottle of Amarone red wine. We had never had it and suggested we have risotto all'Amarone. I could not imagine risotto using red wine but went along with it, and as always, I learned something. Both Laurie and I loved it. Once again, the artistry of the Italians never ceased to amaze me. We finished our work after lunch the next day, and Lidia took us to the train station for the train to Firenze.

We arrived and took a taxi to the Lungarno hotel and ate in their ristorante adjacent to the hotel Borgo San Jacopo. So typical of the Ferragamos. The restaurant was well-designed, one entire wall facing the Arno River with a beautiful view of the city and furnished lavishly. The food lived up to the decor. We left by train the next morning for Rome to spend the night with the plan to fly to Spain. We flew to Barcelona and changed planes for Alicante. We arrived late afternoon and checked into the Sidi Sand hotel. That night, we had dinner at ristorante Darsena and ate paella with seafood. It was incredible. We walked around the town after dinner and once again felt blessed with the weather. It was in the low eighties. Our trip at this point had been everything we had hoped for, and we were anxious for the next phase, getting to the Cidon factory to view Loretta's prototypes and later hooking up with Antonio to meet the people at the belt factory.

CHAPTER 8

Alicante, Spain

I spoke to Mike, letting him know we had arrived in Spain, and he informed me he had received Loretta's expense voucher. "Dad, she flew first class to Barcelona and spent the weekend there. It is ridiculous." I was reminded of the first trip we took with her and Scott to Venice. He had made reservations to stay at the hotel Europa, and I was shocked when we checked out to find the charge was $650 for the one night. Laurie was upset about this latest lack of common sense, the flagrant spending of our money. She said, "Joe, you need to have a talk with her when we return to Chicago. You are too loose. We watch our expenses, and we do not even take a salary to save money. I said, "Laurie, right now we need her, and I will talk to her, but be reminded that they brought us to two factories in Verona we never would have found, so have some patience. I'll get on her about her travel expenses as soon as we return."

Alex from Cidon picked us up, and we drove to the Cidon factory. We were anxious to see what Loretta had accomplished. We were escorted to the sample room. Alex forewarned us that Loretta had ordered a lot of prototype samples. As soon as we entered the room, we realized that was a gross understatement. There were more than five hundred shoes scattered all over the room, on tables, on shelves and on the floor, as many as six colors of a style. It was a disaster! The worst part: there was not one style that fit the Tommy Bahama profile. These were to be prototypes. We could not understand why she had ordered every style in every color. Mariano Cidon, the owner of the factory, walked in as we were trying to make some semblance of order of the mess in the room. He shook his head and expressed his disbelief at what was before us.

He asked, "Do you see anything here that you think you can salvage for the line?" "Mariano, I am really sorry for this, but there is not a single sample that fits the lifestyle of the Tommy Bahama customer. This is a disaster. How much do we owe you for this?" He said, "We have spent close to $10,000." Laurie went into shock. I remained calm on the outside but was boiling on the inside. "Mariano, we want to do business with you, so let's clear this out so we can start all over again for the next line. I do not want to look at this. We will not be able to focus. Here is my proposal. I will make you a promise that we will give you 5,000 to 10,000 pairs for our opening orders for next season. You may charge us one dollar to two dollars a pair extra until you recover your loss for this disaster." He replied, "That works. Let me get someone in here to clean this up." We turned a low moment into a nice understanding.

I said to myself the solution to the problem was sitting right there. Laurie needed to take the ball. She had a better taste level, great design, and style sense. She had the passion for the brand and could sketch. She did well at Sensi, and we had just completed a nice session at Rosetta. It was time. We selected six styles from their Spring 1999 collection, and Laurie started sketching minor changes on the upper parts of them, and we selected colors for each style that were Tommy Bahama colors. As she finished each style, Alex took it back to the factory, and in two days, we had rough but workable prototypes to make decisions. We gave Mariano the green light to proceed and make sales samples.

When we got back to the hotel after dinner with them, I gave Laurie the word. "I am going to fire Loretta when we get back, and you are going to take over all shoe development." The next morning, Antonio picked us up and drove us to the belt factory, where we met the father, son, and daughter team that reminded us of the Sensi family. The father, Juan Jose, the son, Francisco, and the daughter, Margarita, were very close in age to the Sensi trio. The factory was mind-boggling. The floors were marble. The workers wore lab coats;

it was immaculate. We had trouble believing what we were seeing. We moved into the conference room to see our prototypes and spent the next two hours working off leather swatches, selecting colors for each style. Antonio had done a great job. The belt buckles were brass with very stylish designs. All I could think was the contrast of the previous two days at Cidon and the disaster that had greeted us there. This cemented in my mind that our decision to go with Antonio was an excellent choice to not only do belts, but this man was making incredible, well-designed shoes for Mezlan. I knew he could be of use in shoe development. We finished the belt program that day and went to dinner with him. I asked him about visiting shoe factories the next day since our plan was to take the train to Madrid in a couple of days and catch a flight back to Chicago. He agreed and told us he would pick us up the following day. We drove to the town of Sax, stopped at a caffe, and had fresh squeezed Valencia orange juice, a piece of crusty bread loaded with sweet butter, toasted, and incredible cappuccino. We drove to his factory first, and he took us on a tour. It was immaculate, similar to the belt factory. His shoes under construction were like diamonds.

We later visited two other factories in nearby towns, one a men's handsewn facility. It was amazing. The people working were actually hand sewing the upper half of the shoes, and they were truly a work of art. The other two were ladies factories, one making fancy dress shoes, but the other was making shoes that could have possibilities for us in the future. I invited Antonio to be our guest for dinner and he dropped us off at our hotel and agreed to pick us up later. We had a great dinner at La Crispeta. Antonio ordered because the menu was in Spanish, and he insisted we start with Spain's answer to Prosciutto, "Serrano Jamon." We had never had it, and he and I had a laugh.

I said, "Antonio, please try and understand the Italians were curing pork a long time ago. The Medicis taught the world how to cook." He argued, "But we made Jamon better and sold it for less money."

We took a taxi to the train station the next morning and boarded a fast train nonstop to Madrid. We stayed at the Hotel Canalejas Alcala. The hotel manager gave us a city map, and we headed for the famed Prado Museum. My interest in the artist El Greco was always on the list of great works I wanted to see. I was aware of the museum's fine collection of his paintings. His real name is Domenikos Theotokopoulos. He was born in Crete in 1541 and died in Toledo, Spain, in 1614. Most of his art was religious. One of his famous paintings was of St. Francis of Assisi, the patron saint of Assisi. His main claim to fame was the eyes of the people in his work.

I said, "Laurie, look at the eyes. They follow you, regardless of how you switch positions. It is amazing how he captured that part of the face." We continued to walk the museum. We left and walked to the Plaza Mayor, the old section of the city, and stopped for a snack and a coffee. It was vibrant. The sun was shining brightly over the tree-lined streets, and because it was Sunday, the restaurants and shops were loaded with people. We loved the city, and Laurie said, "Next time we come to Spain, let's plan on spending some time in this magnificent city." That night, we had dinner at El Pescatore and had vegetable Paella, which was the best we had had the entire trip. We celebrated it with a bottle of Rioja, and I said, "If Antonio was here, we would be in a debate on Italian reds versus Spanish. I would have to say this is a great red." The following day, we departed for the long flight back to Chicago after a very satisfying trip. I called Loretta the first morning and explained in a very diplomatic way that we were moving on, and Laurie was taking over product development and sent her a two-month severance.

By the middle of June, we received an outstanding thong sandal from China that had a woven upper strap. It had Tommy Bahama written all over it! Laurie had previously sent a sketch of it to Antonio, and he created a belt that centered the exact weave on the middle of the belt. We were extremely pleased with this creation, which was all Laurie. It cemented in my mind that my decision to hand the development reins to her was the right move. In July, Laurie made the presentation of the line for Spring 1999 at the Tommy Bahama sales meeting, and it was well-received. We got kudos on everything, especially the belts. We also were getting close to the regional sales reps and their sub reps. They were helping us get our foot in the door with Sensi with their apparel accounts.

Laurie and I attended the Magic show in August. We now had our own section in the Tommy Bahama show booth. It was a great two-story house. There was no way to describe it. You could not call it a booth. It was an enormous facility, very much like a twelve-room home! Each regional sales rep (six of them) had their own section. There were meeting rooms on the second floor and a private meeting room that was like a conference room on the first floor. All the reps, including ours, had appointments, and the crowds of buyers were lined up the minute the doors opened. At this point, I had been in the apparel business for forty-four years and had been doing trade shows the entire time. I had never seen anything like these crowds.

The show lasted four days, and usually, the people traffic slowed a little on the third day. Not the case with Tommy Bahama. Even the fourth day was busy until the end. It was raucous. These were not lookers. Those people had been well-trained in that they knew if they did not place their orders, they would not get the needed merchandise for the coming season. I informed our salespeople I had been given the word by Tommy management not to take any risks when it came to purchasing inventory. "Buy what you sell, and sell what you buy." They were given the word. "Make sure you tell your buyers if they want delivery of our shoes and belts, they needed to leave their purchase orders at the show."

Laurie had drawn our line sheets, depicting the products by hand. Copies were made for the show and a packet for each salesperson to be used when they hit the road. These were not ordinary drawings. They were drawn with the same blueprint precision for a building. We had shipped the spring 1998 sandals and the sneaker we developed from China, and they retailed very well. That worked two ways. The accounts that had sold them were eager to buy again, but more importantly, it gave confidence to the salespeople and to the Tommy Bahama management.

In September, Laurie and I headed back to Italy, later to Spain. We flew to Milano, spent one day and night, and as always, we window-shopped for ideas. The pressure was on Laurie. This was to be her first complete line development. We paid the traditional respect for the progress of *The Last Supper*, and as always, we were impressed.

We had an early seven o'clock reservation at Antica Pesa, and jet lag got the better of us. We jumped in a taxi after dinner and literally were in bed exhausted by nine o'clock. On Wednesday morning, we caught the early train to Verona. The plan was to spend Thursday and Friday working at the Rosetta factory. Laurie had sent sketches to start the fall 1999 line of women's shoes. Lidia Baldo had suggested we spend the weekend. She wanted to show us the Verona countryside and travel around Lake Garda.

Lidia is a beautiful, warm, friendly, lovable lady. She is tall and bright and has an incredible personality and an infectious laugh. She worked in London for a year after finishing at the university. She was twenty-eight that year, and the business relationship soon blossomed into what has become a lifetime friendship. We love her dearly. She picked us up and took us to the Hotel Victoria and told us she would be back at seven-thirty for dinner. "I am taking you to a new restaurant. It is very casual. I have a surprise for you tonight." The surprise was meeting her boyfriend, Stefano. That night he was very reserved and polite. He did a lot of listening. We did learn he was in the wine filtration business, self-employed, but very little else. We had dinner at Antica Bottega del Vino. The ristorante had an incredible wine cellar, and we had the privilege of seeing it. Stefano knew the owners, and I invited him to order the wines for the evening. I was surprised. He knew every vineyard on the wine list, and he shared information about them. The significant thing was his selection. He chose inexpensive wines that were exceptional. This was once again a lesson. Learn to order wines from the region you are visiting. They are always the best and usually less expensive than the well-known brands from other regions. He and I fought for the check. I won the battle. We liked him. It was to be the first of many dinners with them as a couple. We had a great dinner and concluded the evening with a walk around the shopping area and to the Piazza della Erbe for an espresso. I mentioned the happy crowd enjoying themselves. It seemed there were no problems in the world. Lidia, who is always up, said, "It is always this way in this piazza." I said, "What's not to like? The weather is beautiful. The food, wine, and desserts are complemented by the people." Lidia and Stefano walked us back to our hotel, and the wonderful evening was concluded with mutual hugs. When we got in the elevator, I said to Laurie, "This is the start of a beautiful relationship that will long survive our shoe business." She and Stefano are two of our dearest friends *to this day*. We were impressed the next morning when we arrived at the factory. The prototypes made from Laurie's drawings were fantastic. We both knew this factory was to become important for us. The next two days were amazing in that the minor changes and embellishments we made were sent back to the factory, and within a few hours, we had them back for the final decision to order sales samples. We finished late Friday afternoon, and Lidia took us back to the hotel and said, "We will pick you up at seven-thirty. Is it okay for pizza tonight?" No discussion was needed. We went to a pizza restaurant in a neighborhood outside the city center. The crowd were locals, and the traditional open fire wood burning oven put some of the best pizza we had ever had on our table.

The discussion centered on plans for the weekend. We were going to go to the lake on both days to visit two cities, have lunch, enjoy a casual weekend and put the shoe business on a cloud. Lidia and Stefano picked us up after breakfast Saturday morning, and we went to Sirmione on the lake and had a delightful light lunch with a carafe of local red wine. We walked the quaint, beautiful town. Stefano told us a brief history. The town was founded sometime between the sixth and seventh centuries BC, and the wealthy people from both Verona and Rome had homes there over the years. The weather once again was perfect. It was a great day to be alive. We drove back to Verona late afternoon, and we agreed to meet for dinner at Ristorante Ponte Pietra, right on the river. Lidia had made reservations and told us to be there promptly. "It is very small, and once the crowd arrives and is seated, there is no place inside to wait for an open table." We all arrived at the same time and had an incredible meal. I yielded to Stefano for the wine selection, and as always, he did not fail. I reminded myself to get back to my book on Italian wines when we returned to Chicago. Once again, after dinner, we hugged, and Lidia offered to pick us up in the morning around ten-thirty to go to the lake Sunday morning.

We went to the small courtyard that housed the balcony of Romeo and Juliet. The actual fact is, while it is famous and attracts thousands of tourists, it has no connection to Shakespeare's romantic novel. The house belonged to a family originally called Casa d Giulietta, a wealthy Verona family. A statue of Juliet is in the courtyard. One wall contains years of love note graffiti. The tourists leave thousands of love letters there every year, and a volunteer group answer every one of them. As early as the sixteenth century, Italian writers were writing stories about Romeus e Juliette before Shakespeare's story. When we arrived, it was late Saturday evening, and there was a crowd of both young and older people, many adding to the graffiti and leaving love letters. I had read the brief history of it and wondered how many people took the time to learn the background. I also had read two books on the history of Italy and could not get enough of this small but enchanting country and its overall contribution to the world.

My desire to continue to learn everything about it has never been satisfied. Lidia picked us up the next morning and drove us to Desenzano, another scenic town on the lake. Stefano had another commitment and could not join us but planned to be with us for dinner. This was a larger city, with a lot to see and do, but first, lunch was calling us. We had a seat at a very quaint little trattoria, and we ordered some grilled vegetables for the table and simple pasta with marinara for our second course. Our hunger satisfied, Lidia told us there was an excellent archaeological museum that housed relics dating back to the Etruscan days of Italy. It was beyond any museum of its type we had ever seen. We saw items dating back thousands of years, and I thanked Lidia afterward for taking us on this whirlwind tour of the lake and for giving up her weekend. "Lidia, one day you and Stefano must honor us by coming to stay with us in California." She agreed. We strolled to a castle she had told us about that was humongous. It had the proverbial moat and was in superb condition. We entered and walked around, and all I could imagine was how much money it would cost to build something like this today. Just the cost of the land and location would be prohibitive. That night, we went to the town of Belvedere for tortellini and feasted. I reviewed the wine list with Stefano and asked about vino Rosso. I noticed an expensive red wine, Valpolicella Ripasso, and ordered it. He smiled and raised his head and looked up and blew a kiss to heaven.

With a hand gesture, he said, "It is one of the best wines from the region." I said, "I was aware, but this dinner is on us. Let's try it." Lidia was in a separate conversation with Laurie. Later, when the wine was served, neither had seen the bottle, and they sipped it. I was sorry I did not have a camera to get the expression on their faces. I was wowed. It was as good as any red I have ever had anywhere, and that includes the best Bordeaux. We had three courses of tortellini, and two hours passed. I commented to them, "What a pleasure dining in Italy. There was no rush by the servers. They were not concerned about turning the table to enhance their tip, for there was no tipping. Loud music was also missing, another plus." They drove us back to the hotel, and Lidia offered to take us to the train station the next morning for our trip to Firenze, but I declined and thanked her and Stefano for one of the most excellent weekends of our lives. We parted with hugs, and I noticed a slight tear in Lidia's eye.

On the train to Firenze, I could not help but reflect back on the years, the hard work, the dues I had paid that brought me here. My mind continued to wander back to my mother, my brothers, Carlo and Jim, and the lessons I learned from them. My mom's hard work and dedication to our family was always there. She inspired me to be the person I had become. My brother Carlo's advice was, "Joe, never forget where you came from. You will always be a kid from The Hill. It will help you appreciate things." It was like being in school, and the transition from grade to grade, how we went from the ABCs, to printing, to cursive, to reading and spelling. The steps we learned and studied in math. Many of the business lessons that led me here flashed through my mind. I thanked God for all the help.

CHAPTER 9

Italy with the Boys
April 1999

With the success of the business, Mike and I decided it was time to reward those who had been so pivotal in our success. A trip to Italy was just the ticket. Scott Bechtold and Henry Killian, who had worked with us since the seventies, packing jeans in the warehouse. Scott was my protégé, and Mike and Henry attended their first year of high school together. Henry was our first hire, running the warehouse when we got the Sensi license back in 1994 for the meager salary of $18,000 a year. He was one of our top salesmen. Mike moved him into sales in the Arizona area initially but decided to move him to southern California. Henry wasted no time establishing himself as a force in the territory.

The reward was well-earned, and the trip was set, a blend of business and pleasure as always. The three of them flew to Chicago, and that same day, we departed for Rome. The plan was to spend the weekend. Afterward, Laurie and I would head to Positano for four days. They, in turn, would venture to Venice, and later we planned to rendezvous in Verona. Upon arrival, a van took us to Hotel d'Inghilterra. We immediately took them to the Spanish Steps and into Caffe Greco for an espresso; they were astounded to learn it had been there since 1760!

From there, we walked to the fountain of Trevi, and I gave them a brief history, and we followed tradition and threw the three coins in the fountain. We strolled down to Piazza del Pantheon, and of course, after spending time there, we stopped for pizza. After walking around Piazza Navona, we sat for a beer. We discussed the history of the piazza. I told the story about Bernini and his rival, Borromini, and how Bernini's statue was ready to catch the church when it fell. It was of one those nice days; the bright sun was shining down on us and created a warm feeling for me being there with Laurie, my son, and two guys we felt were family.

Scott said, "Uncle Joe, how did you find time to learn all the history of this city?" "Scott, you have known me for a long time. History is my favorite subject. It satisfies my curiosity about what has happened in the world over the years. I can't begin to tell you how many people I have sent to this country, sharing the sites, hotels, and restaurants. And of course, the knowledge, which makes it special, is much more interesting than what one can get on the internet. You will not find most of those things I just described on the internet. I have kept data in a book on every restaurant we enjoyed, hotels, sites, all recorded by city. Every time I read something special about this country, I put it in the book to be used at some point for some future visit. A perfect example is the restaurant where we are dining this evening. I read about it in *Travel and Leisure* magazine years ago. I first ate there in 1985."

We finished our beer and walked back to the via Condotti and sat on the Spanish Steps, and Mike suggested a photo.

We strolled down to the piazza del Popolo and went into the church, and later we walked up the other end of the street that led to via del Corso and to the hotel. It had been a long thirty-six hours for them with very little sleep on the plane. We agreed to meet in the lobby at seven-thirty to go to dinner. We took a taxi to Cafe Romolo. It is located in the Trastevere area and we dined al fresco. We all had a salad and the same pasta with fresh asparagus. We enjoyed two bottles of Livio Felluga Chardonnay. There was a lot of ribbing going on at Henry's expense by Mike and Scott, "Henry you are guzzling that wine like it is water," he was paying little or no attention to them. We all laughed, including Henry. The next morning, we went to the Colosseum and walked through old Rome. Afterward, the boys took a taxi to the Vatican. They stood in the long line for well over an hour, but finally went in. They were amazed and could not believe Michelangelo painted the ceiling. I had explained he was not a painter and really did not want the job. But the Pope insisted!

I told a story that Michelangelo once took a break and went by mule to see his friend Raphael, who had an apartment above the restaurant where we had eaten the night before, only to find him unavailable. At the time, Raphael was living there with his mistress.

Henry asked, "Joe, are you telling me that Cafe Romolo has been there since the sixteenth century? Was it a restaurant back then?" I replied, "The building was there. I am not sure if it was a restaurant, but why do you find that hard to believe? Yesterday you were in the Pantheon that dates back before Christ was born!" We concluded the day with a visit to St. Peter's, and once again, they were astonished. They were particularly impressed with Michelangelo's incredible white marble statue of the Pieta. That night, we took them to La Pergola, and we ate like royalty. It was cool to share this with them. They deserved it, for they both worked hard for us.

The final day was planned to just walk to various piazzas in the morning, including Campo dei Fiore for pizza at the bakery. We climaxed the afternoon with a visit to Borghese Gardens and museum, where I pointed out some of Bernini's marvels. We had dinner that night at Da Bolognese, and they got a taste of that famed city's cuisine. We had prosciutto que melone (prosciutto with melon) and pasta Bolognese and panna cotta for desert. The boys took the train to Venice the next morning. Laurie and I headed by train to Naples for four days to rest in Positano. We were picked up by our driver for the ride along the Tyrrhenian Sea, and Laurie said, "I will never forget this stunning view of the sun shedding light on the water." For me, I could not help but think back to my first trip to Italy and the Mercedes. That first taste of Italy without plans and reservations. My mind switched back to all the events that allowed us the opportunity to return every year. I tried to recall how many times we had been there and lost count.

We finally were able to get reservations and checked into the San Pietro. Our room looked directly out at the sea. It was lunchtime, and we sat outside and had some pasta. I told Laurie, "This is going to be tough to beat for the rest of this trip." Later, we had Bellinis and watched the sunset. We kept our dinners simple. Two nights at the hotel and two at Donna Rossa.

On the second day, we had made arrangements to take the Hydrofoil to Capri for the day. I had read about a great place for lunch, Da Paulino. It sits in a lemon orchard, and after walking the general area of town, we took a bus up to Anacapri. It is at the top of the mountain and is a separate town. The lunch was out of this world. The bread was homemade and rivaled my mother's. It was warm, and we were told Nonna had just taken it out of the oven. We had her homemade pasta with a light cream sauce that rivaled any Michelin star ristorante! The lemon trees scented the air, and lilac bushes caused conflict with the smells emanating from the kitchen. For dessert, what else? *Fresca crosatata al limone* (fresh lemon tart).

Laurie said, "Joe, thank God you have the sense to write these places down. We never would have found Donna Rossa, and now, here we are in the middle of nowhere, thousands of miles from Chicago in this tiny little town, sitting under a lemon orchard eating like royalty. God bless you!" The four days flew by, and we were back on the train to Rome. We spent the night and left by train the next day to rendezvous with the boys in Verona. Lidia picked us up at the train station and took us directly to hotel Victoria. Mike, Scott, and Henry were already there, and we agreed to go for pizza with her that evening. After dinner, we took them to Piazza delle Erbe for espresso and to catch up on their trip to Venice. The next morning, Lidia drove us to the factory to work with her and Rudy on the spring 2000 line for Tommy Bahama. For lunch, we went for tortellini, and we drank two bottles of wine. Scott remarked, "Do you guys eat like this every day? I am ready for a nap." We worked until eight o'clock that night.

Lidia and Rudy took us straight to dinner at ristorante Ponte Pietra. Once again, the boys were very impressed with the food and wine. Henry said, "Why can't we get pasta like this and vegetables like this in the States?" I explained the Italian pasta manufacturers here do not have to deal with the restrictions of the federal government and the additives put in the pasta in order to ship it to us. As to the fruits and vegetables, the Italians want them picked when they are ripe. Lidia tried to get the check. I caught her discussion with the waiter. My Italian had improved to the point where I had no problem understanding the language so long as people were not speaking too fast. I grabbed the *conto* when it arrived. We finished late afternoon the next day. It was a marathon. The boys were really astounded at what was involved in making a pair of shoes. They had a couple of hours in the factory and watched some of our current line being made. At dinner that night, Henry said, "Laurie, I commend you on what you do. This is a remarkable experience. I have an entirely different attitude about my job.

The next morning, we headed to Firenze for the day, and the boys got a brief taste of it. I had made reservations to see *Michelangelo's David*, and we took them for focaccia. They loved the city. Both Henry and Scott said, "I can't wait to come back here." We had dinner at Ottorino and had seconds on the Fiore di Zucca. We caught a seven o'clock train the next morning for Assisi, and Giampiero and his sister picked us up and took us to the factory. We planned to spend a day and a half. We gave them a tour of the factory, and they watched a pair of sandals being made from start to finish. Both Scott and Henry had sold thousands of pairs. They just could not believe the process.

We had dinner at La Pallotta that night, and the boys ate like they had not eaten that week. I joked, "We just blew the budget for the rest of the trip." But Scott grabbed the check. "Uncle Joe, this one is mine and Henry's." He was taken back when he saw the number. "Am I reading this right? It looks like it is about eighty dollars with two bottles of wine!" We decided to go to Spoleto the next day, a Saturday. It is the home of the famed artist Fillipo Lippi. The Sensis joined us. Laurie and I had never been there. It is a medieval city surrounded by vineyards and olive trees in the Umbria region and is another gem. It dates back to the twelfth century, but I had studied a little history and learned people had been living there as far back as the Etruscans. There is an annual music and art festival that is world-renowned. It was interesting to note we did not see a single

American tourist the entire day. The walls that surrounded the city were astounding. As was the case in most of Italy in the days when inner city wars were threatening; they built those walls to last. It seemed as though they were recently constructed.

We had lunch at a great trattoria and shared many stories with the Sensi family about the marketing we had done to bring the brand back to life. The following morning, we took the fast train to Milano. When we arrived, once again, Scott and Henry could not get over the size of the monumental train station. I gave them a little history about Mussolini. It was a tribute to him. I explained he gets a bad rap for the mistakes he made and is never credited for his achievements. I explained when he took over in 1920, he was determined to make Italy a world power. The economy in the world was rocketing. Not so much the case in Italy. He vowed to change things. First was the railroad system. Trains were never on time. The stations were obsolete, and he made updating them a priority. He began manufacturing newer and faster trains and expanding service to many new cities and towns. Next was the language. The Italians were speaking twenty different dialects. He changed that. The language of Dante became the new national voice of Italy. Children in school had to learn to speak that dialect! Next, he made another major change. Child labor was abolished. Children were mandated to go to school until they were sixteen and could not be hired below that age. He made some serious mistakes. He became a dictator and alienated the people. Then he joined forces with Hitler after he came to power in the thirties and fought against Europe and the Allies during World War II. That was his biggest mistake.

We walked across the street and checked into the Gallia, and got the family treatment. Our rooms were upgraded, and we agreed to meet in the lobby in thirty minutes. We walked to Via Monte Napoleone and window-shopped and ended up in our favorite courtyard at Il Salumaio for lunch. "Uncle Joe, how did you find this place?" Laurie said. "We stumbled on it years ago, and we've been eating here ever since." All the pastas were homemade and fresh. We ordered family style for the table, including prosciutto, salami, and beautiful sliced tomatoes. It was a mini feast. Mike said, "Dad, this one will go down as one of the best meals I have ever had. This is my check." We had reservations to see *The Last Supper* and headed there after lunch. Again, I gave them a little background about both treasures in the room, and they were awestruck. Henry said, "Joe, Mike, and Laurie, we can never repay you for this trip!" I responded, "Henry, you have paid us in many ways since you were a high school kid working in the warehouse." We walked to the duomo and went in, and once again, they were wide-eyed. From there, we strolled across the street to the Galleria and had a coffee. I shared the history of it, and it felt great to share one of the best parts of the trip. We had dinner that night at Antica Trattoria della Pesa and had three orders of the baby meatballs. Laurie convinced the boys to have spaghetti ala erbe. In the morning, I called for a taxi to take us to the airport, and when we jumped in the cab, the driver put on a CD by Van Morrison, and it rocked us all the way to the airport. Later, after we were home for a few days, Mike and Henry sent me the CD. Every time I played it, the fond memories of the trip returned.

Joe with Lidia and Stefano in Verona

Positano

The Spanish Steps left to right, Scott Bechtold, Laurie,
Joe Reina, Henry Killian, in front Mike Reina

CHAPTER 10

Major Advancement of Product Development

Back in Chicago, we started receiving prototypes of shoes from Spain, China, and Italy in the late days of April. Laurie was putting in twelve-hour days communicating with the factories, and we hired an assistant for her. I stayed on the road, working with the reps. Sales were robust at retail and Mike was doing a great job of receiving and shipping new arrivals, including the new belts. He trained both the office and warehouse personnel well, using the knowledge he gained all through high school and college working in our warehouse in the seventies and eighties. We were reordering basic items every week for the Tommy Bahama products. Sales were way beyond projections!

In June, I flew to Dusseldorf for the international shoe fair, arriving late morning on a Thursday, and I walked the show searching for shoe manufacturers and ideas. It was massive and no way to see it all. By Friday, the last day of the show, most of the patrons had left, but I stayed all day. As I was about to leave, I approached a small booth displaying unique leather sandals. I spied a fisherman's sandal at a distance and approached. A man was sitting at the table smoking a cigarette and reading the paper. His show badge read the brand name Vanni and his name was Casare. I introduced myself using my poor Italian and asked if he spoke English. He did not. I showed one of our line sheets and presented my card. Since this was a show to attract retailers, I explained as best I could that we are a significant brand in the states. I asked, *"Saresti disposto a fare sandalo per noi?"* (Would you be willing to make a sandal for us?) He replied, *"Si, ma no discount!"* I laughed and asked if it was possible to meet in his office the next afternoon, and he replied, *"Si dopa pranzo"* (after lunch). I learned his office was about an hour from Firenze, which was my next stop.

I had a meeting scheduled for Monday in Assisi. I flew to Firenze Friday night and called Riccardo, and he picked me up Saturday morning. We drove to the Vanni factory and met the Vanni family. Riccardo spoke at great length about us and the strength of the brand, and my fifteen-year history of bringing Sensi to the US and Japan. There was an immediate change in Casare's attitude. The wife of one of the owners was there. Her name was Patricia Vanni, and her eyes widened when she heard Riccardo's comments. We reviewed their collection and settled on five styles in black and two versions of brown, all beautiful Italian leathers. I promised to send the label and box information. We then went to see the factory, and no surprise, it was immaculate. They took us to lunch in the nearby Tuscan hills. A new relationship was born. These were warm Tuscan people, and it later developed into a family friendship.

On Sunday, I took the train to Assisi, and Giampiero picked me up and took me to the hotel. We agreed to meet for coffee the following morning. I spent the next day with Lorenzo, reviewing the new colors we had put together on our previous trip. I ordered sales samples and caught the late afternoon train for Rome. The next day, I flew back to Chicago, satisfied that the trip to Dusseldorf was time well spent.

In July, we flew to Seattle for the Tommy Bahama sales meeting, and Laurie presented the new shoes for the spring 2000 line and the highlight of her presentation was a new sneaker that had the Tommy Bahama palm tree embossed on the sole and great ornamentation on the upper part of the canvas. In addition, we got applause for the fisherman sandals from Vanni. I showed the new belts, and we received great acclaim for them too. It was a new day for us. We had our reps there and later in a private room at the hotel, we had our sales meeting and showed the new Sensi colors. It was the climax of two very successful days.

When we returned to Chicago, there was a book waiting for me from our good friend in St. Louis, Phyllis Fresta, *Under the Tuscan Sun*. I read it that weekend and later saw the movie. I called Phyllis to thank her and asked her to put her husband, Joe, on the phone. "I loved the book. It reminded me of our many trips to Tuscany, Rome, and Positano. We need to visit Cortona, where Frances Mayes bought and renovated her home, and some of the nearby towns Laurie and I have visited, especially San Gimignano." We agreed to go in 2000.

We attended the Magic trade show in early August, and the first three days were exhausting. The traffic was nonstop. We did not have lunch until late afternoon, and we ate in shifts. The response to the new lines were beyond our wildest dreams. We had three days back in Chicago to catch our breath before leaving for Rome. We arrived in Rome to a blinding rainstorm, and when we got to the hotel, I said, "If we stay here, it will be difficult to stay awake. Let's take umbrellas and walk and proceed with our usual window shopping.

That evening, we had dinner at Piccolo Arancio. We took a train the next day to Bologna, spent the night, and we had a great meal at CIBO Bistro Bolognese. Our waiter at Ristorante Bolonese in Rome was right. The food was outstanding. It is a five-star restaurant. We rented a car and drove to a small town, Reggio Emilia, near Parma and checked into Hotel Posta (it had once been a post office) and had a light dinner in the dining room.

The next morning, we stumbled into an office building that had a sign on the door, "Ufficio Regionale del Parmigiano" (Regional Office for Parmigiano). Laurie's curiosity surfaced, and we entered. There was no one to be seen. She walked around the reception desk and knocked on the door of a private office. A man answered and politely asked in Italian, *"Posso aiutarti?* (Can I help you?). I answered in my poor Italian, "We would like to arrange to see a cheese factory." He understood and showed us on a map where to meet the next morning just outside the city of Parma at eight-thirty. He was there when we arrived, and we followed him to the factory. Upon arrival, he took us to watch the milk being emptied from a truck into copper vats, and we continued each stage of the process. Laurie was given a large spoonlike wooden paddle to stir the milk during the cooking process. I asked the question, "Do you work seven days a week?" He laughed. "Yes, because the cows give milk every day." From there, we watched the maestro form the cheese wheels and place them in salt water. Later they put them in a temperature-controlled room with racking to be stored for two years. He explained they turn the wheels every twenty-four hours. He then called for another man to meet us, and he took a wheel from a rack and tapped it with a small hammer. Then with a special knife, he cut a wedge for each of us. It was the most incredible piece of cheese I had ever tasted. I said, "If I had a loaf of my mother's bread and a good bottle of red wine, I could sleep here."

We could not help but relate the experience to everything worthwhile. To achieve the best in any product, it takes a significant effort, and we must understand this is why we pay the price for excellence! We drove to Parma, another hidden gem, and checked into the hotel Baglioni, one of the nicest chain hotels in all of Italy, and we were warmly greeted. We visited the Cathedral and the baptistery and walked the city. We found the main piazza named after General Garibaldi, who was involved in bringing the city to the unification of Italy. I had read that during Napoleon's reign, France controlled it. Later, we strolled the park, a beautiful tree-lined area that reminded me of the Tuileries in Paris. I also read the city dated back 3,000 years. I tried to imagine what life was like at the time. We had dinner that night at a five-star ristorante, La Greppia Parma, and as always the case, here we were in the middle of Italy, and we stumbled into another restaurant that went into my travel book. We took the train the next day for Firenze and checked in to the Lungarno hotel. We had dinner right there at the hotel restaurant and retired.

Riccardo picked us up early the following morning to go to the Vanni factory and a new ladies' factory. We had been getting calls from the Tommy Bahama ladies' reps for dressier shoes. We went to Vanni first; where Laurie was greeted warmly and we spent the day working on the fall 2000 line. She went into the factory after lunch and met with the two brothers who owned the factory. She watched them make the sandals from start to finish. Riccardo drove us back to the hotel, and we agreed again to an early start the next morning. We had dinner at Il Pizzaiuolo that night and walked around the Piazza della Repubblica and window-shopped. The city was buzzing, and the streets were jammed with people. It was one of those beautiful moonstruck evenings that we did not want to end.

We went to a beautiful factory called Valore the next day and met the owner, Ghisberto, and his son, Stefano. They insisted we see the factory first, and we saw some high-quality shoes being made, including three different styles for Valentino. We went into the showroom, and they presented their current collection. We were overwhelmed. We picked six styles, and Laurie began sketching, and later, we selected various leathers and colors for prototypes to be made. They took us to a great *osteria* for lunch. I made a comment once again about how great the pasta is in Italy compared to the states. We were back at the hotel by four o'clock.

Riccardo later did something extraordinary. When the next shipment from Vanni arrived at the warehouse, there was a case of pasta in one of the cartons. That extra care by that warm man continued twice a year for five years!

On Friday, we had a free day. I had read about another interesting city near Firenze called San Gimignano. After breakfast, we took a bus to the nearest town, then a taxi to get there. It is a walled city that dates back to the thirteenth century. It took us no time to locate the main piazza, Piazza Cisterna. There were many towers, and it reminded us of Lucca. They were well-maintained and looked as if they were constructed last year, but they dated back 800 years. We went into the duomo that was constructed in the thirteenth century, and it too was another tribute to the popes of the period. It took over 200 years to complete. It remains one of our favorite places to visit. I mentioned to Laurie, "Next year, when we come with the Frestas, we must bring them here."

We took a taxi back to the bus station and the bus back to Firenze, satisfied that we found another gem to revisit and share with people we care about. There is no way to describe the joy I get from helping people find their way around Italy. I have lost count on how many we have shared our experiences with. What is especially gratifying is when they return, they share their trip with us. We see their photos, and it enables us to relive those places we love.

We were scheduled to arrive in Verona the next day, Saturday. I had been trying to get my friend Bob Emfield to go to Italy for years, and we finally agreed to meet in Verona since it was our next stop to work. We had a wonderful dinner with Bob, his wife, Laurie, her sister and husband, and his son, Gregg, and his wife MaryJo that night. We walked the town afterward, showed them the Colosseum and walked the shopping area, and ended up at piazza delle Erbe. It ended a very nice evening with them. We all stayed at Hotel Victoria and agreed to meet in the morning for breakfast. I had made arrangements for a van to pick us up at ten o'clock to take us to the lake to see Sirmione.

The weather was beautiful. The sun was exceptionally bright in the solid blue sky when we arrived. Bob said, "There is no way we would have ever experienced this without you pressuring me to come here." We stopped at a pizza ristorante for lunch, and they saw for the first time the traditional open flame, wood-fired oven, and everyone claimed it was the best pizza they had ever eaten. We returned to the van and the driver took us to Desenzano, and as expected, the group marveled at the continued beauty of the lake and surrounding area. Bob's son, Gregg, came up to me while we were strolling the town and said, "I will never forget this trip and the time you put into the entire two weeks for us. The cities, the restaurants, the sites, the hotels, the history—all of it—we have had an incredible time, thanks to you!"

"Gregg, there is no way I can ever repay your dad for pushing Tony and Lucio to award us the Tommy Bahama license and the joint venture, so this is a minor payment in return." On Monday, we went to work at Rosetta and spent two days nonstop. We only took a break to have lunch. We were working on prototypes from sketches Laurie had sent them in June, and they executed her designs perfectly. On the last day, time got away from us. It was seven-thirty, and we were exhausted. Lidia suggested we go for a nice dinner. She took us to our favorite ristorante, Ai Beati, the old olive oil factory and we had fresh roasted fish with vegetables cooked in the same pan with the natural juice of the fish. She ordered the wine, a very nice local white I had never heard of.

The next day, work was completed in time to go to Belvedere for tortellini. Afterward, Lidia took us to the train station in plenty of time for our trip to Milano. We checked into the Gallia and didn't even unpack. We had a seven-thirty dinner reservation at Antica Trattoria della Pesa, had the usual dinner, and we went back to the hotel, having achieved everything we had planned. We were happy to be heading home.

In July, we attended the Tommy Bahama sales meeting in Seattle, and as in the past, Laurie presented the new line, including the belts, to all the reps: she received kudos from everyone. Antonio did a great job of taking her sketches to reality. We had spent a great deal of time with Antonio at his facility in California on both belts and footwear, and it showed in the product and later in sales.

We had a brief sales meeting with our reps and headed back to Chicago. At the August Magic trade show, we heard from our Seattle rep that the lead buyers from Nordstrom for belts wanted a meeting. They were there bright and early, and we showed the line. We gave them six belts for their meeting with the rest of their buyers across the country. This was not the only highlight for the show. Fred Mossler, a former Nordstrom buyer, and Tony Hsieh were at the booth that same morning; I knew Fred. He told us about a new business they were starting called Zappos. The plan was to sell footwear and related footwear products on the internet. They asked if we would be willing to sell them both Sensi and Tommy Bahama. We gave them an approving nod and showed them both lines.

Before the four days finished, the Nordstrom belt buyers all came by and dropped off very nice orders, which put us in every store across the country! In September, prototype samples were arriving every day. Laurie was working from sun up until nine to nine-thirty at night. I had to drag her out of the office to go to dinner. We received a call from a young lady, Leanna Krie, who recently moved to Chicago from New York, where she had been employed by a shoe company. We interviewed her, hired her on the spot and put her to work the same day. We immediately took a liking to her. She was single and had the same work ethic we had. There was no clock in Leanna's office. She was cute, twenty-seven, and full of energy. She knew a lot about the shoe business, and she adapted to our way of thinking immediately. We learned her favorite hobby was pool and billiards. One night after dinner, we went to a pool hall near our house, and I challenged her to a few games. She cleaned my clock!

The sales meeting for the fall lines was in Palm Springs. I requested an audience with the Tommy Bahama partners and their CFO. We were constantly struggling to pay our suppliers. Both of us were factored by CIT financial services. We borrowed money from them on our inventory and receivables. They were very flexible with us because the companies were connected, and the CIT principals had known me for a long time. Tommy Bahama had opened quite a few stores, and they owed Paradise Shoe Company a lot of money every month, and because of the tie-in, we were not able to borrow against those receivables. We were still operating with the original $250,000 we put in in 1997, and we agreed to put in another $250,000 each. The next day, we had our sales meetings, and once again, the improvements in the products were met with great enthusiasm. Sales for Sensi reached $2,900,312 for the year, and Paradise Shoe sales doubled the previous year's sales and profit, significantly higher than our projections. But the real surprise was advance orders for spring 2000 surpassed total shipments for 1999! This was the basis for going to the partners for additional capital to fund the business.

CHAPTER 11

April 2000

I was struggling for time to do everything that needed to be done to handle the increased business. It was an insane growth well beyond the high numbers we had projected.

Mike Reina and I decided to call a sales meeting in Phoenix. The plan was to make a few announcements and get the sales force on the road. I opened the meeting by naming Mike as our new president, thus taking over marketing. I knew this would cause some concern about nepotism.

I kept it simple and explained that Laurie and I were on the road. Between working with Antonio six times a year in California, the trade shows in Las Vegas four times, the trips to Italy and Spain twice a year, the sales meetings, my role as CFO and the purchasing of both Sensi and Tommy Bahama, there was no time to be involved in sales. I stressed Mike had done a great job getting us into the spa business and he was a partner in the business.

With a tear in my eye and an emotion-filled voice, I turned the reins over to him.

Mike made the following announcement. "We feel people follow the sun in winter, starting in October, and it is important the stores have new sandals and new colors. Tommy Bahama has a holiday line for apparel, and we are going to show some new Tommy Bahama footwear that can be shipped in July or August, which will pick up our business at a time when we usually struggle."

Laurie made the presentation showing both brands of the new arrivals.

Mike came back with the next exciting announcement. The newly opened Arizona baseball stadium had a swimming pool overlooking the entire stadium that could be rented for each game. He had arranged for management to include Sensi as a sponsor and provide a giveaway as part of the rental agreement for the pool. Each attendee would receive a pair of Sensis! That would grant us national exposure at the games and on TV. We celebrated the success with a company dinner at a great pizza restaurant.

We flew to Milano and spent the day doing our usual routine. We had an early dinner at the hotel.

Our next stop was Verona. As in the past, Lidia and Rudy were well-prepared and had executed Laurie's designs to near perfection. A few styles were so well done we gave the green light for a small order to proceed and manufacture them at once for delivery to our warehouse in late October, which helped our business in November.

We moved on to Firenze the next morning. We needed two days there and stayed at the Savoy. The city was booked solid. We had reservations at our two favorite restaurants, Ottorino and Buca dell' Orafo. Both were loaded with people, including many tourists.

Both factories were well-prepared, and we had shortened days. The styles needed very minor changes. We did have great lunches with the two families. The relationships were fast becoming family.

The next day, we departed for Assisi. We allotted one day there for new color selections and arrived late in the morning. Giampiero took us straight to the factory, and after greeting everyone, we reviewed how well they interpreted Laurie's colors.

We all went for pizza that night, and once again, we were with family. It never ceased to amaze me what we had achieved. All the people now welcomed us at every factory with open arms and great respect.

We took the train to Rome on Friday and spent the night at the Hotel d Inghilterra and had dinner at Cafe Romolo. Lilac bushes surrounded the tables in the garden and the aroma of marinara sauce filled the area. We took a leisurely walk in Trastevere. The beautiful September weather highlighted a long day, content with our accomplishments during the week.

We flew to Barcelona for the weekend and stayed at the Hotel Art. It had been built for the Olympics and had a well-earned five-star status. Once again, I had done my homework and studied the city and a little history. We visited the Gaudi Cathedral, which began in 1882 and was still under construction, Laurie's architectural profession surfaced, and she explained a lot of Gaudi's design qualities. We went to the Picasso museum and later another museum that housed much of the art of Joan Miró. That night, we had paella at Tickets, a very nice four-star restaurant.

We walked the old part of the city on Sunday with no agenda and enjoyed the sunny day, stopping at a local Tapas restaurant for lunch, and we had dinner that night at a fabulous restaurant called Disfrutar Barcelona. We enjoyed a series of small plates. First, a tasting of a crusty shrimp dish loaded with garlic and butter, next a purée of baked eggplant, and finally fresh fillet of fish, with a very light cream sauce. That really topped the trip food-wise.

On Monday, we flew to Alicante. It was back to reality. Alex picked us up, and we went to Cidon. Mariano greeted us warmly, and we reviewed the collection they prepared. Once again, we were delighted. I mentioned to Laurie that 2001 would double the previous year's sales, based on what we had seen at the factories for the past ten days.

Antonio had asked to pick us up the next morning at six-thirty for the two-hour drive to the belt factory. After stopping for orange juice and a piece of Spanish crusty bread and coffee, we went to the family homecoming with our friends at the belt factory. They were ecstatic at how many belts we were selling. We had exceeded the projected number I promised Antonio.

What a pleasure viewing the fruition of our work with Antonio in his office. The belts we designed were great. I selected four and placed orders to be in our warehouse by mid-November. We had lunch together and finished the rest of the day in Antonio's office.

Bob Emfield had sent us a boat shoe he had purchased in June while in Ireland, and we showed it to Antonio. It was late in the afternoon, but he made a call to a nearby factory, and we drove to the next town and met the owner.

We showed him the shoe, and he agreed he could make it. In a matter of two hours, Laurie and Antonio made drawings and changes that no longer resembled the shoe. The owner told us molds would be required for the sole, and we agreed to an additional cost for them until he recovered his cost. He promised a prototype in four to six weeks.

CHAPTER 12

Opportunity

With the frenzy of business activity, the heavy travel schedule to Europe, coupled with the sales meetings and trade shows, Laurie and I were exhausted.

We flew to Palm Springs for a weekend to rest, with a plan to drive over to Huntington Beach for a few days to work on product development with Antonio for the spring 2001 line and later to drive to Las Vegas for the Magic show.

It is well-written that people with vivid imaginations never really sleep. Their bodies rest, but their minds are always working. My mother was the epitome of this, and I inherited it from her.

I had heard that the partners at Tommy Bahama were not happy with the current licensee for hosiery. This occupied my mind the entire weekend. When we woke up that first morning, Laurie asked, "Did you sleep well?" I said, "No. What do you do before putting your shoes on? You put your socks on, right?"

"Joe, I have not had coffee. What is it now?"

"I am going to find out who is making the Mezlan socks for Antonio. And I am going to see if we can get the sock license."

When we arrived at Antonio's office, I went right to the shelf and picked up a pair of socks and asked him, "Who is making these, Antonio?"

"His name is Michael Tolaini. He has a small factory in Brescia, Italy.

They make socks the old-fashioned way with hand-linked seams on the toe and heel. Why do you ask?"

"I want to get the sock license for us from Tommy Bahama. Can we call him?"

We reached Michael, and after a brief conversation, he agreed to meet us at the Magic show, and my next call was to Bob Emfield to set up a meeting with Tony and Luccio for the first day of the show.

The meeting with Michael lasted less than thirty minutes. He presented a few pairs of his socks, and the partners promised to get back to us with a decision. I went for coffee with him and Antonio. Michael and I returned to the booth, and we walked him through some of the Tommy Bahama apparel, then showed our footwear and belts. Before he departed, I explained that Laurie and I were heading to Italy in early March, and we agreed to spend a day with him. He said he would work on a few designs for our arrival. He took a Tommy Bahama apparel line sheet with him.

Prototype products began pouring into the office, and Laurie and her assistant, Leanna, were working twelve-hour days. Included were eighteen sock samples from Italy. The styles were split between sport to be worn with shorts and those for casual dress. The apparel company was selling more silk dress slacks than cotton. These socks had no labels, no packaging whatsoever. Laurie began designing the labels.

"I have to go to New York to meet with Tony Margolis to get his approval before we go another step. Laurie, we have enough here for you to take a half pair and start designing labels. We have five weeks before the sales meeting to get everything together."

My meeting with Tony went well. He approved ten of the eighteen and gave very good suggestions for improving those he rejected. I called my travel agent and booked a flight to Milano two days later.

Michael Tolaini picked me up at the airport and drove to his office. After working nonstop (except to eat) for two days, and into the evening, we completed the changes. I was back on a plane for Chicago, confident that we would secure the license.

As mentioned earlier, I believe in the big book up there somewhere that a page turns every day in our lives. Once in a while, something eventful happens. Most of the time, it is routine, and we are simply lucky to be alive.

Sometimes, we must open the door to wake up old man opportunity from his nap. We are forced to kick the door down and proceed on our own to control our destiny! This sock challenge was our chance to enhance our product mix.

Laurie finalized all the label designs, which included fiber content, and suggested retail prices and a great name, Luxe, to be associated with the name on each style. She sent the designs to Seattle for the company responsible for all labeling to get them proof ready for Italy.

We had three weeks left to complete the collection before the Tommy sales meeting. Everything arrived two days before the meeting, and we were overjoyed at how well Michael Tolaini followed through. The packaging was the cream on the cake and incredible. We had requested a seven-thirty meeting with Tony, Bob, Lucio and the lady in charge of licensing. Mike Reina also joined us. Laurie showed the collection. The anxiety was beating the three of us all through the presentation. It was quiet, and everyone was waiting to hear Tony's comments. The tension was so thick you could cut it with a knife!

Tony looked at Laurie and me and said, "I was not at all pleased with our former licensee. These socks enhance the brand. Congratulations. Looks like we are in the sock business."

We turned our own page, thanks to Antonio and Michael Tolaini.

We flew back to Chicago, and Laurie continued to prepare her sketches and ideas for the spring 2001 line and sent them off to the factories. The list had grown. Scott Chin handled everything for the China factories, Lidia for Rosetta, Riccardo for the two in the Firenze countryside, Giampiero for Sensi, Antonio for belts and shoes in Spain, and Alex for Cidon. We had put together a great team and injected the Tommy Bahama passion needle deep into their veins.

In early March, we flew to Milan, spent the day on our typical quest of searching the stores, and later dropping by for our never-ending curiosity regarding *The Last Supper*. We took a taxi back to the hotel for a rest and after dinner at Antica Trattoria della Pesa, we retired early.

We took a train to Brescia, and Michael Tolaini took us to the sock factory. It actually was part of his family home. He introduced us to his wife, daughter, and son. We reviewed his collection and a few ideas he had put together and made a few selections for him to make some prototypes. After lunch, he took us to the train station, and we departed for Verona. Lidia picked us up in time to go to dinner. We had a simple dinner at a small ristorante near our hotel and retired early.

In the morning, Lidia took us to Rosetta to work with her and Rudy. They had all our prototypes on display when we arrived. We explained we had a busy schedule and wanted to try to complete everything by the end of the next day in time to catch the late afternoon train to Firenze. We worked until eight-thirty, broke for dinner, and went to Belvedere for tortellini. As always, we delighted in the trio of incredible delicacies.

The next day was highlighted by a beautiful floral fabric they had found. It was as if it was designed by the staff at Tommy Bahama, and we were overwhelmed. Rudy had taken two of Laurie's sketches and used the fabric on the uppers of them and came up with sure winners. We went ahead and ordered sales samples for everything. I was so sure of the two floral shoes that I placed an order for them to be shipped as soon as possible. We were told they could be in our warehouse in sixty days, and I knew Luccio would put them in the Tommy Bahama stores immediately. Being able to deliver new product, in season, to the stores set a pattern on many key items that had improved our business.

We caught the four o'clock train to Firenze and arrived in time to go to dinner. We had reservations at Buca dell'Orafo, and as in the past, we had a great dish of pasta, a small carafe of red wine and retired. We were exhausted.

Riccardo picked us up early the next morning, and we went to Vanni. They had also taken Laurie's ideas to fruition and were well-prepared. With minor changes, they revised the samples and were ready for us when we returned from lunch. We enjoyed being with Casare and Patricia. Her warm feelings for us always made us feel like we were family.

The revised sandals were perfect. Again I placed some orders to get them to us in June, which traditionally was a slow month. I knew we could rely on the company stores to take part of the order. We returned to Firenze with time to walk the stores and shop, always keeping our eyes open for possible ideas and additional color direction.

That night, we needed our fix for Fiore di zucca at Ottorino. We were there early, satisfied our addiction, and had a great plate of spaghetti Bolonese.

The following morning, we went to the Valore shoe factory and met with Ghisberto and his son, Stefano. It was a pleasure viewing their interpretations of Laurie's advanced designs, and we were impressed. We made color selections on six prototypes and ordered sales samples. Later on, they took us to their favorite ristorante in the Tuscan hills. As always, neither of us discussed business. I asked them about their favorite towns in Tuscany, restaurants, sites, and history questions and made notes. We planned a tour of Tuscany with our dear St. Louis friends, the Frestas, once our work was finished.

We went back to the factory and completed all our notes and final photos of the prototypes and drove back to Firenze. We walked to the Piazza della Republica and had an espresso to wake up. Jet lag had caught up with us. A good lesson here: try not to take long afternoon naps. It can cause you to wake at two in the morning and toss and turn the rest of the night. We had dinner that night at Giacosa on via Tornabuoni, an excellent ristorante. We enjoyed a bottle of Pian Della Vigne Brunello, and I must admit, it was a toss-up as to which was better, the food or that bottle of wine.

We caught the early train for the three-hour trip to Assisi the next morning, continuing what seemed like a long drawn-out journey. We were both satisfied as to what had been accomplished. I complimented Laurie. "Your organizational skills have made the nightmares of the past a pleasure in the development process."

She replied, "The team you put together at every level has played to our success. We had the same team in Phoenix. Mike had a well-organized warehouse staff and an incredible administration group. The best part was he came in under the budgets I set for all expenses. The hard-working dedicated sales force completed the team."

"That being said, I think we deserve a raise. For the past two years, only Mike has taken a salary from Sensi. It's time the three of us start taking a salary from both Paradise Shoe and Sensi. Plus, let's set up a bonus predicated on profit from both companies at the end of the year."

Giampiero Sensi took us to the hotel Umbra and agreed to meet us the next day at Caffe Sensi for coffee. We had dinner at La Pallotta, and all I could think of was the many times arriving in my sister Josie's basement and the greetings from family members that had not seen us for a year. We were home, we got our greeting, and now we can sit and eat.

Once again, Giampiero was ready for us, not only with the samples that had the colors Laurie had suggested, but he had two new sandals. One was a thong that was unisex and a slide model for women where the upper strap was modified from the top-selling model for men. They both were winners; we selected colors for both, and I gave him a small order to get production started.

The next day, Phyllis and Joe Fresta arrived at the factory for a tour, and we made the introductions to the Sensis. Afterward, we took them to the Basilica of Saint Francis of Assissi and then showed them Piazza Minerva, the main piazza of Assisi, and walked the old area around our hotel. That evening, we had dinner at La Pallotta.

The next morning, Giampiero took us to Perugia, and we rented a car. Joe agreed to drive the entire trip and drove us to Siena. I explained a brief history about the city, the city's annual Palio, a horse race held twice a year in the Piazza del Campo. It is a highly competitive race between towns in the Tuscan hills.

Piazza del Campo dates back to the early Roman days, and at that time, it was the Forum.

It was time for lunch when we arrived. We sat at a small *osteria*, Tullio ai Tre Cristi outside, right along the piazza, and Phyllis commented on the incredible weather. It was everything we could hope for. We had great pasta and shared a salad for the table.

We went to the duomo afterward and walked the town, which sits atop three hills overlooking the Tuscany countryside. We completed our tour and drove to San Gimignano and checked into the Hotel Collegiato. It was minutes outside the walled city. We did not unpack. We went to dinner at La Vecchio Mora. This was a marvelous find, recommended by the hotel manager as her favorite. We decided to order for the table: two pasta dishes, one risotto to share, and a ravioli. I suggested a bottle of Chianti, and Joe complimented me on the wine selection. The restaurant went into my book.

The following morning, we went right back to town and walked the general area around Piazza della Cisterna. Laurie and Phyllis walked up one of the towers. I explained a little history of the walls surrounding the town that dated back to the thirteenth century.

We decided to go to Cortona, the site of *Under the Tuscan Sun,* the book Phyllis had sent me. Joe parked the car at the bottom of the hill, and we walked up to the city center. It was love at first sight. So cool to be in this incredible tiny village.

We browsed the shops. Joe and I went into a wine store and checked out the wines. We both were astounded at how low the prices were. Joe commented that he carried some of the wines in his restaurants and said he paid more than two times the price wholesale for what they were retailing.

I was shocked at how clean it was. Not an inch of graffiti anywhere. None of the people were speaking English. It did not resemble a tourist town.

It was noon, and we were getting hungry. We decided against a big lunch, mainly because we did not want to spend two hours. I suggested we find a shop to make us a panini, and we found a cheese store that sold all kinds of cured meats.

I asked the man who greeted us, *"Puoi fare un panino que salumi e formaggio?"* (Can you make us a sandwich with salami and cheese?) He smiled and said, *"Sei Siciliano!"* (You are Sicilian.)

I laughed, and in my bad Italian, I replied, *"Sono Americano, ma mi madre, mio padre sono nati in Sicilia."* (My mother and father were born in Sicily.) There is no doubt I murdered my response, but he got the message. "Make us four good sandwiches."

He pulled out a large piece of focaccia and cut four nice-sized pieces. He cut them open, drizzled olive oil, sliced the salami so thin you could read a newspaper through it. Then he took two balls of fresh buffalo mozzarella, sliced it thin and laid two pieces on each sandwich. Next, he took a beautiful ripe tomato, put two slices on each, threw a little salt and pepper on them, put the top piece on and wrapped them separately. I asked for the *conto*, and it came to ten dollars! Needless to say, there was no need for a Subway sandwich shop in the town.

We walked across the street and sat on the steps in front of the church, and $1000 would not have bought one of those paninis from us.

We drove to Arezzo next and walked the city center and found the magnificent Piazza Grande.

We entered the Duomo San Donato, and Joe Fresta stated, "Joe, I have been in more churches on this trip than I normally visit in a month."

"Joe, go stand outside. Let's absorb a little culture." We laughed.

I had read about the archeological museum and suggested we step in because it had artifacts that dated to the early Roman days, but it was closed. We stopped by the Casa del Vasari, which at one time, was a palazzo and found it hard to imagine what it would cost to build such an incredible building today. It housed beautiful frescos and art treasures worth millions, and there was hardly anyone in there.

It was getting late, so we drove back to the hotel. When we arrived, our wives went to the room, and Joe and I went for a drink outside by the pool. Joe asked, "Joe, how did you find this hotel?"

"It was recommended by a friend who had stayed here. It dates back to the sixteenth century. It was originally a monastery owned by the church and I put it in my book a few years ago."

We had dinner at the hotel and retired early. It had been a long day.

At breakfast, we discussed the next few days and decided to go to Volterra and Pisa that day.

Phyllis was gracious about the trip and thanked us for the time we put in making it possible.

I replied, "This all happened because you sent the book *Under the Tuscan Sun.*" Speaking of the sun, it was a glorious sun-filled day—no pollution, very typical throughout Tuscany.

The drive to Volterra was through the Tuscan hills. It was every photo and movie scene we had ever witnessed. The rolling landscape was dusted with villas that steeped the imagination, and one could only wonder about how many generations they had been passed down.

We arrived in Volterra in time for lunch. We went to Ristorante Del Duca and spent two hours. Toward the end, I commented jokingly, "Joe, do you ever wake up, shake your head and find it hard to believe where we have come from; looking back to those early days on The Hill? We did not have two nickels to rub against each other, and here we are in Volterra, spending this kind of money on a trip in Italy."

"Are you kidding me? Never in my wildest dreams. Think about when we were kids. Nobody traveled to Italy. How many times have you and Laurie been here?"

"I have lost count. We are fortunate that business brings us here two or three times a year, and we try to visit one region at a time to avoid spending too much time on trains. We never tire of the Italian people, the history, and culture. And let's not forget the food."

After lunch, we drove to Pisa and did spend quite a bit of time at the Leaning Tower. Then we walked the city with no agenda. That night, we had dinner in San Gimignano at Valentina Capodori and ate family style. Later, when Laurie and I were back in our room, we talked about how easy it was traveling with the Frestas. Laurie asked, "How long have you known Joe?" "A long time, fifty-six years. He lived four doors down the street from me with his mom and grandmother, who were great friends with my mother. We were inseparable as young kids."

The next day, we drove to Parma. Laurie and I had a lunch meeting with our freight forwarders from Firenze, and we asked the Frestas to join us. They suggested Trattoria Corrieri. It was so good it made my list of favorites. After we dined, the four of us walked the city, and the Frestas were really impressed. At the end of the day, we checked into the Hotel Baglioni.

Next on the list was Santa Margarita. In the early planning of the trip, we reviewed a map of Tuscany, and one of the cities we all agreed we should visit was Portofino. Laurie had never been there, and I had not been back since 1980.

We arrived in Santa Margarita late and checked into the Hotel Imperiale Palace, and agreed to meet shortly in the lobby. We had dinner reservations at Le Cupole. We walked the city center afterward and found a very fine caffe. Joe and I had an espresso, and we called it a day.

We took the train for Portofino the following morning and a taxi to the town center, and we strolled along the water. Phyllis said, "I can't believe how lucky we have been. The weather has been remarkable." I said, "Phyllis, I prayed for this weather, and my prayers have been answered."

Joe said, "Joe Reina, you are so full of it." He got the Reina look. We all smiled.

We walked up to the Hotel Splendido and strolled through the lobby and then the grounds.

Joe Fresta asked, "Joe, why aren't we staying here? This place is incredible."

"Joe, three nights here and you would have to dig into your first communion money you have been stashing all your life to pay the bill. We are going to have lunch here."

We moved to the beautiful Terrazzo for lunch overlooking the city and the sea, and the maitre'd approached us, and in practice, I said, *"Abbiamo una prenotazione, il nome e Reina."*

Joe Fresta again had to pull my chain. "Joe, why didn't you just tell him we had a reservation?"

"Joe, I am hopeful he will realize I am Sicilian and be somewhat intimidated and ensure us good service and great food." The girls laughed.

"This is Liz Taylor's favorite hotel, and she loved coming here with her many husbands."

We searched the menu, and when the waiter arrived, I asked his favorite dish. He said the lasagna was made in-house. I turned my nose up and said, *"Ma pasta in il forno,"* with a question mark expression "pasta baked in the oven."

He laughed and said, *"No solo pasta, con marinara.* Just pasta with marinara sauce."

We looked at each other and gave him an affirmative nod.

We were served a mini appetizer of fried baby artichokes, sautéed in butter and a taste of garlic, compliments of the chef. And then we were served the meal of the trip: simple house-made wide pasta noodles made with the best sauce I have ever tasted. I have sent numerous people for that lunch over the years and have always received extreme gratitude. The view of the sea, the atmosphere, the smells emanating from the kitchen, and wine set a mood never to be forgotten!

To avoid the taxi and the train ride, we had no schedule, so we convinced a man with a small boat to take us back to Santa Margarita.

We drove to Milano the next day and tried to get in to see *The Last Supper*, but the church was closed for renovation. We went to the duomo, crossed the street, and showed them the Galleria. From there, we went to Via Monte Napoleone and had lunch at Il Salumaio. The weather continued to favor us, and we walked the entire area after another great meal.

We concluded the trip our last night together at Antica Trattoria della Pesa and shared several items on the menu.

The Frestas had an early flight the next day. We were staying one more night, so we said our goodbyes when we returned to the hotel. Both thanked us for a great trip.

I said, "Listen, we were on the same trip. We enjoyed being with the two of you, so it was a pleasure for us too."

For us, it was a warm feeling to have shared our experiences with two dear friends and it was well worth the time and effort spent planning the adventure.

Laurie and I took the train the next day for Lago di Garda and spent a relaxing day with nothing to do. We walked the town and saw a sign, "Forno a legna per pizza." Even Laurie could interpret that sign, and it was pizza for lunch.

We took the train back to Milano and later had a Bellini in the bar before dinner at Il Bagutta near via Monte Napoleone.

We flew to Chicago the next day, satisfied with our accomplishments for the year, anxious for the arrival of the prototypes we had worked on during the trip.

Phyllis and Joe Fresta at the Galleria in Milan

Phyllis and Joe Fresta in Cortona

The author with Phyllis and Joe Fresta at La Scala in Milan

Joe Reina and Joe Fresta in Tuscany

Joe Fresta in Milan

Joe Reina, Phyllis Fresta, and Laurie Reina at the Duomo in Milan

Phyllis Fresta in Assisi

Reinas and Frestas in San Gimignano

CHAPTER 13

Team Structure 2001

Laurie and I were pleased with our progress on the new sock designs and labels and were excited to see the boat shoe, but there were a few more hoops to jump through. The jury was out, and there was always anxiety until we received store approval with orders. This was especially true of the boat shoe price.

We flew to Naples, Florida, for a licensee meeting and met with the new director of licensing. Laurie's intuition surfaced. "This woman is going to be a pain in the ass." We spent two boring days. She knew little or nothing about the brand, and it was apparent that she was in way over her head about products represented by the small group of licensees at the meeting. This was especially true about men's shoes and belts, and I commented to Laurie, "How are we supposed to get direction from this woman about product development?"

We flew directly to Los Angeles and took a taxi to Antonio's office to work on the spring 2002 line for belts and shoes.

He showed us the sole for the boat shoe. It was perfect and surpassed our expectations. Once again, Antonio showed how important he had become to our group.

We sat with him and designed two uppers for it, one a lace-up and the other a slip-on. We moved on to belt design and did four new ones based on suggestions we had received from stores and salespeople.

Antonio said, "You did more belt business this past year than I did with Mezlan. Juan Jose is thinking of making an addition to his factory. Do you think the business is going to continue to grow like this?"

I replied, "Tell him to be careful, Antonio. I can't guarantee that."

The following morning, we completed our meeting in time to go to lunch, and Laurie and I rented a car and went to Palm Springs for the weekend. One of my golfing partners, Bill Randolph, was a sailor, and I showed him the boat shoe bottom, and he loved it. He said, "When I sailed, a good boat shoe was in the $250 to $300 price range. How much will this sell for?"

"I have no idea, Bill. I will learn that when we go to Spain in the spring."

He said, "I want to buy a pair as soon as you make them."

While we were there, Laurie designed a sales rack for the stores to display belts on one side and socks on the other side. It had the Tommy Bahama name and logo at the top. It was a beauty. We sent it off to Seattle to have the label people give it official approval and have a prototype made.

The following week, we drove to Las Vegas for the Magic trade show. We were inundated with the crowds. The orders left no doubt 2001 was to be another big year.

In March, we departed for Barcelona, spent Sunday evening at Hotel Art, and caught a flight to Alicante the next morning. Antonio had invited us to stay at his home, and we left at six-thirty the next morning for the belt factory. Our four new belt sketches turned out perfectly. I wrote an order for the belts to be shipped in sixty days. The plan was for our salespeople to start selling them as soon as they received sales samples.

We proceeded to the factory making the boat shoe and were amazed at the two styles.

Antonio had been there earlier working with the factory. We were so pleased we added two colors on each style, and I gambled and ordered sales samples and fit samples to be sure they fit before placing a purchase order. We were a little shocked at the price. I did a quick retail price calculation and found it would have to sell for $175 in the stores.

We flew to Barcelona and changed planes for a flight to Rome, and our driver took us to the Hotel d'Inghilterra. It had been an exhausting few days, and we decided to spend the weekend relaxing with no agenda. I told Laurie, "I am going to cut Spain down to one trip a year. Same for Sensi and Assisi. Antonio can handle Spain product development, and we only need a spring color change for Sensi."

On Monday, we took the train to Assisi and went directly to the factory, and began working on color changes for each style. We worked all day, only broke for lunch and worked into the early evening. Our plan was to take the morning train to Firenze and change trains for Porto Ercole, a small town on the west coast of Tuscany. We took a taxi to Il Pelicano, an all-inclusive resort on the Tyrrhenian Sea, for a well-earned rest.

We arrived at this extraordinary hotel, which far exceeded what we heard from friends who had stayed there. It sat on top of a large hill overlooking the sea. Our room faced the Tyrrhenian Sea. The manicured grounds were like a park, and the facilities included a saltwater pool, a fitness room, a well-maintained garden, and the weather topped everything. It was splendid. We went for lunch in one of the two restaurants and enjoyed some really good pasta, which the waiter told us was house-made. We changed into bathing attire and headed for the pool. It took me about ten seconds to fall asleep.

That night, we had dinner in their gourmet restaurant, which had a well-deserved Michelin star. For dessert, we enjoyed for the first time Gorgonzola cheese with Castagna (chestnut) honey. Laurie said, "I feel like I died and went to heaven."

I replied, "This is only a slight reward for those twelve-hour days and six-day work weeks."

We concluded our weeklong stay and ordered a car to take us to the train station for our trip to Genoa to change trains for Milano.

It was a Sunday. When we arrived, we learned of a train strike. There were no train employees working, and we had no choice but to have the driver take us to Genoa.

We finally arrived at the Gallia in Milano in time to go to dinner. We missed lunch, and our appetites were beyond description. We ate at the hotel, and the food was luscious.

We window-shopped around Via Monte Napoleone, paid our visit to see *The Last Supper*, and headed back to the hotel.

The next morning, Michael Tolaini drove us to the factory in Brescia. He surprised us with a very fine collection of new socks, and all we had to do was color them. At the end of the day, he drove us to the Hotel Savoy, and we had dinner at a nearby Trattoria and called it a day.

We took the train for Verona the following morning. Lidia met us at the train station and took us to Rosetta, and they were also well-prepared. All of Laurie's sketches had been well-executed, and it cut our usual two to three days down to one and a half. We had dinner both nights with Lidia, who was becoming a faithful, warm friend. Our relationship with her had long ago drifted from a business one. We loved being with her, and once we left the office, our business was never discussed.

We departed for Firenze the next day and checked into the Lungarno and went to Ottorino for dinner.

We left early with Riccardo for Vanni the next morning, and they showed us two new sandals that were slip-on styles, and we immediately approved them. They were outstanding, and we gave them initial purchase orders for both.

On Thursday, we went to the Valore factory. Here too, they were well-prepared. Our time was reduced to one day to complete the line. That night, we had dinner at Cibreo, a restaurant I had read about in *Departures* magazine. We had baked eggplant mousse for an appetizer and fusilli pasta with a ground veal sauce. That was the best meal since leaving Il Pelicano. For dessert, we shared a round doughnut-shaped baked pastry filled with hot chocolate, which satisfied my sweet tooth. It was a piece of art. We decided we needed to take a long walk. We very rarely ate that much food. During our walk, we both agreed Cibreo should go into my travel book. I had a separate page for each city we had ever visited, with hotels, both those where we stayed and outstanding ones I had read about. Same for restaurants, which included our favorites and future ones we needed to try.

We boarded a train for the long ride to Rome the next morning, stayed at the Inghilterra and decided to try another new restaurant, Piccolo Arancio, near the Trevi Fountain. Even though it was in a tourist area; we had great pasta and shared a delicious veal chop.

The following day, we flew to Chicago.

We went to the office on Sunday to catch up on mail and messages before Monday's onslaught of phone calls and faxes. I told Laurie, "Now that the factories in Italy are so well-organized, when we go in the fall, let's fly to Milano on a Saturday, arriving Sunday morning and do what needs to be done. On Monday, let's catch the early train to Brescia, work on hosiery with Michael for one day, and go to Verona the next day. Spend two days at Rosetta and head to Firenze, and finish the week. If necessary, we can work Saturday. Since we need not go to Assisi or Spain, we can take a few days to relax and go to Forte dei Marmi."

We worked diligently in preparation for the next sales meeting in July. Prototypes were pouring in from all the factories, and we needed an additional assistant for Laurie. We put the word out that we were hiring. I was struggling to find time to do the buying and chasing the money to pay the factories. We hired a woman who had been laid off when Florsheim was sold, and she turned out to be the help we needed. She assisted both of us with the day-to-day workload, taking a load off Laurie. The business was reaching insane increases for Tommy Bahama, and Mike was constantly on my case because we were running out of basic belts and certain Tommy sandals and sneakers. There were days we didn't have time for lunch.

A prototype of the fixture Laurie designed for belts and socks arrived. One came to our Chicago office, and one went to Phoenix. The cost was $120 each, but we could get it down to $100 if we ordered 500 units, which we opted to do.

In July, we attended the Tommy Bahama sales meeting, and Laurie and I presented the new lines. The hit of the presentation was the line of boat shoes. Bob Emfield was beaming. After all, it was his idea. He was very gracious in praising us for executing the shoe he had sent us. There was some concern about the price because of the retail price of $175; Bob stated the one he bought and sent to us was $300.

In August, we returned to the Magic show in Las Vegas and worked with several major Tommy Bahama apparel stores. We enjoyed seeing the reaction to the products. The boat shoes were well-received, but the apparel stores voiced some price resistance, same from the shoe stores. They placed orders for them in small quantities and told us most of the boat shoes in the market were $100. They admitted our shoe was higher quality, there was no comparison, but they thought the consumer might balk at paying $75 more.

In late August, we exercised our plan and flew to Milano on Saturday and spent the day, unable to get into the Gallia. It was booked solid. We stayed at the Manzoni hotel, which was good, but the Gallia is hard to beat. We window-shopped Via Monte Napoleone and went to the Gallaria for espresso to try to stay awake. We tried a new restaurant that night called Al Buon Convento, family-run, nothing fancy. The decor was understated and not the least bit crowded. We ordered simple food: roasted fresh vegetables to share and ravioli con zucca (ravioli stuffed with pumpkin). It was perfect for our moods. We were tired, having been awake thirty-one hours, and went to bed exhausted.

The next morning, we took the train to Brescia and spent the day working with Michael on socks. We had been getting requests for more novelty socks with palm trees and pineapples, themes from the Tommy Bahama Hawaiian shirt collections, and Michael had prepared them for us with unique embroidered prototypes.

We checked into the Savoy hotel and had dinner at an excellent ristorante, Al Vogt, a beautiful five-star dining room; I had read about it in *Vanity Fair*. We elected to eat outside. It was one of those incredible calm evenings. We could hear the waves on the lake. It was a clear night, and there were a billion stars flooding the sky.

We chose to have the chef roast a whole fish and fresh vegetables for us in the open-fire wood oven and made a note to be sure to return. It went into my book.

Michael drove us to Rosetta the next morning and joined us for lunch in Belvedere for tortellini.

Lidia and Rudy were ready for us when we returned to the factory. They updated some of the best-selling shoes currently in the stores, with new uppers, and had prototypes of Laurie's sketches, which we reworked. The shoes were incredible, especially the sandals that embellished the floral and fruit designs taken off the Tommy Bahama ladies' print tops.

That night, we went to Pizzeria Bella Napoli, quite a contrast from the previous night's fancy dinner, but nonetheless very satisfying.

We finished the next day in time to catch the late afternoon train for Firenze and checked into the Lungarno in time for dinner. We ate right there at Borgo San Jacopo, while it is the hotel ristorante, the food and service is rated as good as any in the city.

We drove to Vanni the next morning with Riccardo and reviewed the new prototypes they had executed from Laurie's sketches, and we added three more sandals to the line for 2002. Sales had been running forty percent ahead each season on their sandals because Nordstrom had put them in all their stores. Tommy Bahama was opening stores all over the country, and Vanni was well-represented in every one of them. We finished early and went to lunch once again in the hills of Tuscany, much to our delight.

We were doing so well financially. My mind began drifting about the possibility of buying a villa somewhere in the area. I was fantasizing of entertaining family and friends, cooking, and having a car to drive to the quaint villages in the area. But the dream faded once we arrived at the restaurant. The thought of everything involved in getting there, coupled with how busy we were, put the idea out of my mind.

Riccardo drove us back to Firenze and dropped us off near the Ponte Vecchio, and we walked to Via Tornabuoni and strolled for a while. Laurie was going in and out of some of the shops. My mind was a million miles away, back to the early days of being in the apparel business and how far we had come.

I was sixty-five years old. Most of my friends were retired. I thought about our travel schedules. We were spending eight months on the road, to say nothing of the stress. I thought about my dream to retire at fifty-five and move to Palm Springs to play golf every day and enjoy life.

Laurie walked out of the Tods store and looked at me. "Where are you right now?" I didn't respond. I knew she and Mike were young and eager to continue the meteoric growth of the business and this once-in-a-lifetime opportunity to be part of Tommy Bahama. It was the greatest success story in the apparel business ever, at least in my lifetime. I buried any thoughts of retiring.

We finalized our business trip to Valore the next day and chose three new shoes for the next line release. We went to lunch with Ghisberto and Stefano, which always made the trip more enjoyable. It was like coming home to visit friends. That friendship was more significant than the business. The two-hour lunches, great food, and wine made the whole experience and travel time to get there worthwhile.

When we returned to the hotel, Laurie worked at the hotel computer. I called Mike to catch up on any product needs, which took us until dinnertime. We had an early dinner at Ottorino and took a short walk to Perche No for gelato and returned to the hotel to pack.

We took the early train to Forte dei Marmi the next morning for five days and had a well-earned rest. We checked into a new hotel recommended by my friend Joe Farinella called Villa Roma Imperiale, a small boutique hotel a short distance from the beach and a nice two-mile walk from the city center. I had asked them to book dinner reservations for all five nights. We didn't bother unpacking. We walked to al Bocconcino for pizza and later took a nice walk around town. The sun beat down on us, and it was a "welcome home" feeling, no appointments, no early wake-up calls, no phone calls, no demands of any kind for five days of bliss.

We took a short taxi ride one morning and went to Pietrasanta, a small town just north of Forte, and discovered another gem. In reading about it, I learned Michelangelo contracted his marble dealings there. It sits at the base of the Apuan Alps. The old part of town has the typical square, Piazza Cello Statuto, with a beautiful duomo and unique shops. We walked most of the city center and stumbled into Fillipo, a Michelin-starred ristorante for lunch. It was early, and we had the pleasure of meeting Fillipo, who introduced us to the head chef, Andrea. When he heard we were from Chicago, he told us he had a cousin living there and gave us her name. We were given the VIP treatment. After we ordered a glass of wine, all kinds of delicacies began to arrive, compliments of the chef, including the best home-made bread we had had the entire trip. We had risotto Milanese for lunch and ate enough food that it necessitated another walk around town. We were stuffed. We never had lunches like that. We were both very diet conscious, but we did not want to insult the chef.

The ensuing four days flew by, and I told Laurie as we boarded the train, "Next time, we stay here at least a week." Forte became our latest Shangri-La.

The train ride this time was from a nearby town called Via Reggio and lasted three and a half hours to Rome, and we checked into the Inghilterra. It was time for our usual trip to Trevi Fountain, and we threw three coins in the fountain and strolled to the Pantheon and Piazza Navona. When we arrived, Laurie challenged me to a coin toss to the columns from the top of the Forum, and we agreed to toss three. We walked the short walk and reached the top and agreed I would throw first, and my coin landed perfectly on top of the column base! Laurie missed all three times, and of course, I gloated all the way back to the hotel.

The next day, we boarded the flight back to Chicago, having completed another successful trip to our favorite country.

There was a mountain of calls and faxes when we went to the office Monday, and reality set in. We dug into them and began preparing for the next sales meeting which was in Palm Springs. We loved that because we could stay in our own house.

Mike called with great news. Nordstrom wanted 130 belt and hosiery fixtures for their stores. In some cases, there would be one in the furnishings department and one in the sportswear department. I said, "Mike, in the thirty years I have been selling that store, I have never seen a brand-named fixture in their stores. This is a first. More significantly, this is better than any advertisement we could run. It is daily advertising and a tribute to the brand."

He replied, "You better check our inventory on belts. They are carrying eight belts from us, and we are expecting a huge order from them for the holiday."

The days leading up to the sales meeting were hectic. There was not enough time in the day. We were lucky to have two dedicated assistants in the office who were putting in ten—and twelve-hour days. Frequently, I would pick up lunch for us, and we always took the women for dinner at night.

We finalized everything with a couple days to spare and headed to Palm Springs a few days to catch our breath and relax before the meeting. There was a dinner party at the Tommy Bahama store and restaurant the day before the meeting. Laurie was not feeling well, so I went alone. I arrived and went to the bar and was about to order a drink. Tony Margolis was at the opposite end with Bob Emfield and Lucio, and he beckoned me to join them. When I got there, he put his arm around me and said, "You are a true warrior of the road! Where is Laurie?"

That compliment was tantamount to having the president of the United States pinning the Medal of Honor on me. I felt like I had arrived in Tony's world.

The meeting was a great success, the lines were well-received, and there was little doubt we were headed for another banner year.

The second day, I was not feeling well, so I didn't attend the meeting. Late in the day, Mike called and said, "Dad, Tony was really upset with the Tommy reps because they were doing a lousy job selling accessories and the other license products, and he threatened to turn everything over to another firm to sell them. That would really put our salespeople in a bind to have to deal with another sales group."

I immediately called Tony and voiced my opinion that it would be unfair to our reps. They already know the buyers at the Tommy apparel stores and all the shoe buyers, and I pleaded with him to give our reps an exclusive for our products. I said, "The last thing I want is to have another group selling our products." He agreed and said, "Okay. Your guys get the entire line for all accounts."

There was no doubt this would really increase sales. Our salespeople were hungry, and it later proved my initial thoughts.

The year 2001 provided a forty-eight percent increase in revenue and a fifty-two percent increase in profit for Paradise Shoe Company.

CHAPTER 14

Continued Growth 2002

We decided to expand our sales force to handle our new responsibility of calling on the retail Tommy Bahama accounts. It was a major job to service the entire country, including Hawaii and the Caribbean islands.

Laurie and I spent New Year's Eve in Palm Springs and later drove to Huntington Beach to work with Antonio on the next line release. Always looking for new information about Italy, I read a great article in American Airlines magazine by a writer who had taken his fiancé to Rome. They had gone to Mass on a Sunday at St. Peter's, and after, they walked to Campo de Fiore and stumbled into a small restaurant called Ristorante da Pancrazio. The five-page article vividly described the place, the food, and an interesting story about a discovery in 1922.

While the building was under construction, a state archeological team revealed that most of the area of the piazza was built atop Pompey's Theatre, which was believed to seat 40,000 people. I tore out the article and saved it, and told Laurie about it. With her architectural training, she'd find it fascinating. Meanwhile, we had to solve a pressing problem.

The cost of the boat shoes was still an issue that we had to resolve.

We broke the news to Antonio that we were taking the manufacturing to China. "Antonio, we can retail it for $100 as opposed to $175 and make a higher margin than the one we are making in

Spain." We showed him prototypes. He examined them and said, "This is a well-made shoe. This is no problem."

Out of respect for his continued assistance on improving and adding new designs for it, we granted him the same commission we were paying him for making it in Spain. While on the surface, it appeared to be a gift, I took all things into consideration as to his overall contribution to our success. He was watching over both belt and shoe production in Spain, which eliminated one trip a year for us. He was inspecting production before our products left the factories, thus eliminating the need to have an agent. He traveled back and forth to Spain and never charged us for travel expenses. He was a trusted and valuable associate well worth the commission.

We drove to Las Vegas for the show and attended an early meeting with Mike and our sales group, which was all about the expected turnout and scheduled appointments with the apparel stores. We were astonished at the orders showing sixty to seventy percent increases over the previous year's shipments. I had taken a page from my Arrow Shirt Company days and prepared for the reps 2001 dollar shipments by category for each store, so it was easy for the rep to review what each store had spent the previous season. Scott Bechtold came up to me at the end of the first day, "Uncle Joe, that paperwork you provided regarding what the stores bought last year was key to getting the orders for next season. It really helped the store and me make their buy." I received the same response from the rest of the reps. My twenty years in marketing at Arrow was better than a Harvard PhD. What I learned could never come from attending class.

Following that success, we drove back to Palm Springs and spent the next two weeks working on our respective responsibilities: Laurie sketching and sending them to the various factories, and me the never-ending job of inventory control and juggling money to pay the factories.

Once again, we drove to Vegas for the International Shoe Show. Scott Chin, our agent, and product development team leader from China came to meet us and worked with Laurie. As did Lidia from Rosetta and Alex from Cidon and Antonio was back from Spain with the prototypes of our January work. They were frenetic, ten-to-twelve-hour days nonstop that provided a significant head start on our next trip to Europe. We were so busy I did not have a chance to watch what was happening sales wise in the booth. At the show, our bookkeeper had totaled the orders each day, and by the end of the third day, both Sensi and Tommy orders had doubled last year's sales. We were on a roll.

In March, we flew to Alicante to work with Antonio.

For the next three days, we stayed with him and worked at the factories on prototypes of the sketches he and Laurie worked on at the shoe show. I placed purchase orders for current needs and for a few of the new styles.

Mike called to inform me that we had received huge reorders for belts from Nordstrom and Zappos, and I placed a major order for them.

We flew Alicante to Barcelona, changed planes for Rome, and checked into Inghilterra in time for dinner. We had dinner at La Campana, our first time. I had read in *Travel and Leisure* that it was the oldest ristorante in Rome, founded in 1518. Laurie said, "That sounds impossible. Do you really want to try it?" We did and had fried baby artichokes, and Fiore d Zucchini stuffed with ricotta. Later, Pasta al Norma that was as good as what we had in Sicily. Needless to say, that ristorante went into my book!

Friday morning, we took the train to Assisi, and Giampiero drove us to the factory. We worked until seven-thirty, and after checking into the hotel, we went to La Pallotta for some bruschetta and a bowl of pasta and retired.

We spent half a day finalizing work at Sensi and took the afternoon train to Firenze and checked into the Lungarno. Sunday was a day of rest. We walked the city with little concern about anything. We soaked up some sun, eating up the solid blue sky.

We kept dinners simple, Ottorino the first night, Taverna Branzino the next, and Borgo San Jacopo at the hotel on Tuesday. We worked at Vanni and Valore, and their preparedness was great. Both teams put great prototypes on the tables, and we were overwhelmed, but not surprised. Great teams are not born. They just don't appear one day. This was the culmination of four years of hard work and having passion for the brand. The same of our entire organization. It was true at every level, down to the latest hire in the warehouse and office.

Next, Laurie and I headed to Milano and changed trains for Brescia to work the season's hosiery line and Michael was ready for us. He invited us to dinner with his family, and we finished right on schedule the next day, and he drove us to Rosetta. The plan was to spend the weekend with Lidia and Stefano at the lake.

We were astonished when we saw the new shoes, another case of teamwork. Artists are famous for improving with every new canvas, and our dear friends had outdone themselves.

I said to Laurie, "Our spring 2003 products will surely continue the incredible revenue increases we have been experiencing." She replied, "How in the world are we to continue to top this?"

As planned, we finished on time Friday to go to a very fine restaurant with Lidia and Stefano for tortellini called La Borsa up in the hills overlooking the city. It had originally been operated by the grandparents of the current owner, a striking lady who Lidia introduced to us. We learned she had made tortellini for the Pope, and Lidia insisted she show us the photo of her with the Holy Father.

Once seated, Stefano ordered a great white wine, Vernaccia Di San Gimignano, and soon the first course arrived. Lidia had explained the dough is so thin that the cooks in the kitchen have to be extremely careful when they remove the tortellini from boiling water so as not to break them. The first course was served in very clear vegetable broth. On the table were house-made thick bread sticks that were addictive.

The second course arrived with a very simple marinara sauce. The servings were from a large platter to us individually. There was more left in the platter on the table. Laurie and Stefano had seconds.

The final serving tortellini platter was stuffed with ricotta and finely chopped spinach, and a mild cream sauce.

As agreed upon earlier, we spent the next two days on the lake, and finally, after two weeks, we relaxed, our time well-spent completing the lines for European products for the 2003 line. We only had to work on China products when we returned.

On Monday, we headed to Rome, arriving late afternoon, and checked into the Inghilterra and walked to Ristorante Maricicianella for a great ravioli dinner for our last night.

Our flight back to Chicago was without incident, and we found Scott Chin had performed his duties well when we got to the office. The prototypes were exactly what we anticipated, so well done, especially the new boat shoe designs, a new sandal, and sneaker. They had success written all over them. We ordered sale samples, and I placed a purchase order for the boat shoes and the new sneaker. This aggressive method of buying with anticipation was bringing fresh product to our warehouse in the May to June period. It provided our sales team the ability to get new merchandise into the stores during those months when most stores were selling leftover spring or summer price reduced stale merchandise.

In July, we attended the Tommy Bahama sales meeting in Seattle, and our product lines once again received rave revues.

In August, the Magic show activity was as it had been the previous show. We were busy; it was almost nonstop the first two days. We worked accounts until six-thirty both days. Once again. orders placed by the stores showed a forty-five percent increase for the same period the previous year, ensuring 2003 was going to be an outstanding year. We again worked with Antonio and the rest of the European team in attendance.

In September, we prepared for the next trip. It seemed like time was out of control. We had been back four months, and it was time to head to Rome. American Airlines stopped their direct flights to Milano, so from Rome, we planned to take the train to Firenze, on to Verona, and then to Brescia. We completed the trip in a week as planned and ended up in Milano after working with Michael on socks. We had never been to the south of France and caught a flight to Nice the next morning.

We rented a car and drove to the Grand Hotel du Cap near Antibes on a beautiful sunny Sunday afternoon. We were fortunate. It was drawing close to the end of the season, and this was before it became a Four Seasons managed resort. I was unpacking, and Laurie picked up the room service menu and asked, "How much is ninety-six francs?" I said, "About fourteen dollars. Why?" She replied, "We will not be having room service. That's how much a cup of coffee and a croissant is." "Well, we never order room service anyway. This place is notoriously expensive, but it is a great hotel, and we will probably never be back, so let's enjoy the week. You know what is facing us when we get back to Chicago."

We took the opportunity to shop for ideas, which was part of the plan. We started the next morning and drove to St. Tropez and bought some espadrilles made in Spain. They had floral material uppers on a rope-type bottom, and the box showed the manufacturer. The plan was to send them to Antonio for possibly the next line. We had lunch at a seaside restaurant called Chez Camille. The fish was actually still alive when the server showed it to us. He said they get their daily fish right when the boats come in! We finished the afternoon shopping in Cannes. That night, we drove back to Cannes for dinner and had pizza at a small pizzeria run by some people from Napoli. The next morning, we drove down to Antibes and stopped in a bakery for two croissants, then walked to a cafe for cappuccino. Our waiter said it was perfectly fine to eat them with our coffee.

We walked around town and window shopped but found nothing. We drove to St. Paul de Vence next and again found nothing, but we did find a very interesting restaurant where struggling artists, over the years, would sketch and leave their art for food, that art was displayed on the walls. One in particular was a Monet. It was called *Le Medieval.*

Driving back to the hotel, I turned to Laurie. "I am going through pasta withdrawal. Let's go for Italian tonight." Back at the hotel, we decided to relax by the pool. There were no chaise lounges. A pool attendant brought two thin mattresses for us, dropped them on the floor near the pool, and asked for what turned out to be forty dollars in francs! I was astounded, but that's the price you pay to stay at that hotel. Laurie grimaced. "Never again." We found a very quaint little bistro in Canne called Gusti Italiani for pasta run by people from Bologna, which satisfied my addiction.

The next day, we drove to Monte Carlo and walked all over town and found quite a few inspiring women's sandals and shoes.

We had lunch at Les Perles de Monte Carlo, which just about broke the budget. We had a simple piece of fish fillet and roasted vegetables and a glass of white wine. It cost ninety dollars and there was a twenty percent food service charge added to the bill!

We spent the last two days laying around the pool on our forty-dollar mattresses and checked out, happy that we experienced the Cote d'Azur, but I said, "I think we should stick to the Italian Riviera and stay on budget."

While we were waiting for our flight from Nice to Paris, we discussed the cost of the trip to the Riviera, and Laurie asked, "Can you expense any of this week?" I said, "No, I will not do that. It is not fair to Mike to charge it to Sensi, and I never want to leave us open for criticism from the boys at Tommy Bahama. That is not my style. We don't need to shop this part of the world anymore."

Business that fall continued to reach heights above our projections, putting tremendous pressure on me to keep inventory flowing on key reorder items. Tony Margolis' statement regarding inventory control was constantly echoing in my mind. There was no way I was going to tell him we were overbought. I was not about to have to sell off any product because of an overstocked position.

The December sales meeting was in Palm Springs. At the company party, Laurie mentioned that Paul Fine, the New York regional sales rep for Tommy, had challenged Leanna to a pool contest after the dinner. Word had circulated that he was quite good, and the betting had already started. It was the sales reps from the apparel company versus the shoe reps, and the more people drank, the more raucous the behavior became. The shoe business and the apparel business was no longer on anyone's mind. This was war!

Margolis saw the steam heating up and signed the check, and we poured into vehicles and drove the short distance to the pool room. It was eight ball, and it had to be banked. That meant that the player shooting for the win could not shoot the ball straight in. It had to be bounced off one of the bumper sides into a pocket.

The tension in the air was intense. There was loud applause when one of the players sank a ball. It seemed like an eternity passed before the table was cleared, and both were trying to put the eight ball away. They were not leaving any bankable shots. Paul finally had an opportunity. He shot too hard, and the ball careened down to the far end of the table, leaving Leanna with what appeared to be an impossible shot.

The tension mounted as she walked around the table and studied the shot. There was dead silence as she returned to make it. We were all holding our breath as she drew the cue back and fired. The eight ball bounced off three sides of the table and headed slowly for the pocket. It went in, and everyone screamed. It was one of those David and Goliath moments!

CHAPTER 15

Living the Dream 2003

We approached the New Year with cautious optimism. Orders in house for the first quarter exceeded the first six months of 2002 by thirty-seven percent. Mike and Laurie were very enthusiastic about the coming year, but my memory of 1980 and the disastrous meteoric rise in interest rates by the idiots at the Federal Reserve were indelible in my mind. Never in the history of the US had we had a prime rate of twenty percent. The economy crashed, and we had one of the worst recessions in our history.

In the late nineties, the Fed did it again. They raised the rates too fast and too high, and the stock market crashed and dropped nearly a trillion dollars! Once again, Tony Margolis' warnings echoed in my mind: "I don't want any inventory problems, Joe."

Mike was constantly pushing me to order more basics, and I continued to closely watch the weekly sales and maintained what I felt was a conservative approach to projected sales.

My attitude was to let the stores miss a few sales. That will keep them hungry. There was no magic formula on the future of the economy.

We flew to Southern California to meet with Antonio prior to the February Magic show and spent three days with him working on the spring 2004 line and agreed to meet him in Las Vegas after the show to give him reorders to take to Spain.

We flew to Rome and checked into the Inghilterra.

Saturday took us on our usual tour of our three favorite sites, and from the Piazza Navona, we taxied to Campo dei Fiore to the restaurant I had learned about from the article in American Airlines magazine, Da Pancrazio. The open fruit and vegetable market was full of people shopping for their weekend food needs, and after an inquiry, we found the ristorante and chose a table outside. It was a perfect day for dining alfresco.

The most interesting thing about that piazza was how important it was to the neighborhood. Not only were housewives shopping; the restaurant owners were there too. Most of the fruits and vegetables had been picked ripe the preceding two or three days. In the afternoon, the fruit and vegetable market folded. The ristoranti opened for lunch. People came in droves, children played in the piazza, and at night, there was a third transition. The ristoranti were jammed with people. These were locals. Rarely did one see a tourist. On occasion, a local band would be playing. This was a classic example of the lifestyle of the people in Italy.

The American Airlines article showed the chef preparing ravioli con spinaci (spinach), and we opted for it. We later showed the five-page article to the waiter, and he brought over an elderly lady, who had been seated with some people at a nearby table, and introduced us. She was the owner and had never seen the article. We asked if it was possible to see the recovered section of Pompey's theatre in the area below the restaurant, and she agreed to escort us after our lunch.

For the record, Pompey was a very important general in the Roman army and rose to power because of his many conquests and battles with Caesar.

Construction of his theatre was started about 62 BC and completed in 55BC and could house an estimated 40,000 people. According to early records, it occupied what is today most of Campo dei Fiori.

The lady escorted us down a winding staircase below the restaurant to the excavated ruins of the theatre and we were amazed at the partial columns and felt like we had just stepped back in time 2,000 years! Laurie stated, "It is so hard for me to imagine a facility large enough to house 40,000 people considering the lack of big machinery." When we returned to our table, a waiter served espresso and panna cotta, compliments of the owner, for giving her the original article from the magazine. I had an extra copy at home.

We departed for Firenze the following day and checked into the Lungarno, and had a very nice dinner that night at Cibreo. We took our customary walk around the city center and were astounded at the crowds. It seemed like the world had ascended to Firenze.

Riccardo took us to the two factories the next two days, and we found our hard work and preparation paid off once again. The prototypes needed very little change, and we ordered sales samples. I placed reorders at both factories.

We completed the rest of the trip on the following Friday in Verona and spent another delightful weekend with Lidia and Stefano at Lago di Garda. On Monday, we took the train to Rome and flew back to Chicago, confident we had a great start on the spring 2004 line.

The first quarter sales numbers were outstanding. We were up forty-one percent over 2002! There were certain belts, socks, sneakers, and sandals that were outselling the basic stock plan I had set up, and the factories were having trouble fulfilling our orders. The salespeople were on my case with complaints almost daily. But I suspected Mike had put them up to this. I decided to raise the basic inventory minimums slightly but was determined not to accede to the pressure by putting us in any jeopardy.

We were well-prepared for the July sales meeting, and the line was well accepted. At a meeting with Tony, Bob, Lucio, and their controller, we reviewed 2002 sales and the six months ending June and agreed to put another $250,000 into the business. There was no opposition.

The rest of the year went smoothly, with no serious complications, and thanks to the spa business, Sensi had a modest sales increase, and Paradise Shoe ended up with a twenty-two percent increase in revenue and a twenty-seven percent increase in profit.

2004 Shocking Surprise

Laurie and I took a ten-day trip to Maui shortly after the New Year and returned to the mainland to commence work with Antonio, and we completed the early development for spring 2005 shoes, belts, and golf shoes before leaving for Magic.

Nothing out of the ordinary happened at the show. We were very busy and were happy with early spring bookings, but the increases were nowhere near what they had been the past three seasons. I discussed this with Mike and told him I was concerned that perhaps we may have peaked. I was going to reduce our basic inventories by twenty percent, and he agreed. I had another concern due to the Federal Reserve raising interest rates. I had a history of the prime rate since 1930, and there was a pattern; every time they raised the rates too fast and too high, a recession or depression followed.

Sales for the first quarter proved me correct. We had only a slight increase, and without discussing it with Mike, I dropped the basic inventory on shoes, belts, and socks another 10 percent.

We spoke to Antonio and decided to forgo the trip to Spain, confident Antonio would complete what we had worked on, and we agreed to see him sometime in early May to see the prototypes.

We departed for Italy in late March, with a plan to work diligently in Assisi for one day and two days in Firenze, allowing for travel to Brescia for a day, and as was the previous trip, a day and a half in Verona. We completed the plan with no interruptions and took a train on Friday from Verona to Firenze. We had a two-hour layover there to board a train to Forte dei Marmi.

We spent six days relaxing and sunning for a chance to get ready for the return and stress to continue developing products for the next sales meeting and shows.

We returned to Chicago mid-April and learned from Mike there was an incredible spurt in business, and we had run out of most basics.

"Dad, I don't know what has happened. We have received huge belt reorders from every major store in the country. Same for sneakers and sandals, both the casual ones from China and those from

Vanni. Please get on the phone, place orders with the factories, and tell them to FedEx the reorders. Pay the extra freight, but get me back in business ASAP!"

I spent the next two days frantically working on the reorders. I called Antonio, who was still in Spain, and he agreed to jump on the belt orders and promised they would go out in a week. Laurie called China and got them to rush orders for both the sandals and the boat shoes. They promised delivery within ten days, and we agreed to their requested surcharge on the boat shoes. The freight share was $1.25 a pair, but we had such a high markup I did not give it a second thought.

My next call was to Riccardo. I told him to go to Vanni and put the heat on them. We had given them so much business over the years, it was our turn. They also performed a quick turnaround and shipped 1,800 units by FedEx. We needed to fill current orders and shipped another 3,200 units by sea to get us back to our basic inventory.

On May 1, Mike called. "Dad, have you heard the news?"

I said, "What news?"

"Tommy Bahama has been sold to Oxford Industries in Atlanta! We have new partners."

It took a few seconds for me to come out of shock. I knew Oxford. I had done business with them in the seventies and knew they were a public company. Public companies usually do not like to be involved with private firms, strictly from an accounting standpoint. This change in ownership meant having audited inventories, and I would have to answer to some CFO.

I was happy for Tony, Bob, and Lucio, but the sting for us was doom. This was the beginning of the end. There was no way I was going to have some bean counter in Atlanta telling me how to run the business!

I had a brief discussion with Laurie about it, and she too was shocked, and she asked, "What are we going to do?"

I said, "We need to sell the business." She was stunned! She said, "Maybe it is the right time. How much longer do you want to be jumping on and off airplanes and working these crazy hours?"

I called Mike back later in the afternoon and gave him the news. "We need to go to New York and sit with Tony and come with a plan to sell Paradise Shoe Company."

I thought for sure Mike would argue with me, but he agreed. I called Tony and told him I had spent twenty years working for a major public corporation, and after being in business for myself, there was no way I could go back to corporate life, and he invited Mike and me to meet the following week.

Tony opened our meeting with the news that he had discussed the sale with the CEO of Oxford and had the name of a firm in Boston that specialized in mergers and acquisitions. We placed a call to his contact and began the process of doing a virtual presentation of the company.

We left the next day and agreed not to publicize the intent to sell. Mike called the plan Operation Bamboo. He handled the entire project, and within ninety days, we began entertaining inquiries, but, nothing was happening. We did not receive a single offer.

I had an unrelated concern. The Fed, in a matter of two months, raised the prime rate another quarter of a point.

This was a red flag, and I laid awake at night unable to get 1981 out of my mind and the late nineties and the disasters that followed. There was no concern in the media about this. The economy was still flourishing, but my brain was working overtime.

I did not say anything to Mike and Laurie. I did not want to panic them, but quietly I decided to slow down the train on purchases, fearing the impact on the economy should these rate increases continue.

In July, we went to the sales meeting in Phoenix and performed our usual responsibilities, and everyone was pleased with the Spring 2005 lines. Our development team had completed their duties on product well, and the reps told us that they felt 2005 would continue to be another great year. But for me, the thrill was gone. All I could think about was concern about the sale and the impact on the economy by the Fed.

The fear was that if the economy took a hit in the coming year, it would definitely impact the sale of the business. There was concern about the apparel company too and how the sale to Oxford would affect it.

We had no offers. There was an inquiry by a belt company, another from a hosiery firm, but nothing from the shoe world.

We still had an obligation to keep the ball rolling. We met with Antonio before Magic and left for Italy right after the show.

Rome was crowded when we arrived. It was challenging to walk the streets. I told Laurie, "It's the economy. People are making so much money that they are traveling abroad, and it was no different at our favorite sites. At the fountain of Trevi, the line to the water was thirty deep. We had to buck them to get down to throw our coins over our shoulder.

We found the entrance to the Pantheon so crowded we didn't go in and proceeded to the pizza restaurant and they were eight deep there. Piazza Navona had even larger crowds.

We went to Firenze and spent a day and a half at Vanni and Valore, but it was difficult putting our heart and soul into the product.

We continued our trip to complete the lines in Brescia with Michael and broke the news to him about the sale of the apparel company and held back about our possible sale. Once again, he was kind enough to drive us to Verona.

It was great seeing Lidia, and we had dinner with her both nights. We did share the possibility of our interest in selling our company, and she promised to keep it quiet.

We returned to Chicago and once again learned sales had slipped in the third quarter. That cemented my mind to slow purchases, and a little bit of fear entered. The last thing I wanted was to have a prospective buyer come along and have to take a heavy markdown on inventory.

Things settled down toward the end of the year. Business picked up for the holiday, and my concern subsided. We ended up hitting our projected sales and profit numbers for Sensi and showed a twenty-one percent increase in sales revenue for Paradise Shoes and a nineteen percent increase in net income!

Below Ristorante Da Pancrazio in Rome, ruins
of Pompey's theatre (Photo 1)

Below Ristorante Da Pancrazio in Rome (photo 2)

CHAPTER 16

2005

I kept my conservative mindset in early 2005 and did not project a significant increase in sales. Mike and I decided to play a wait and see game until the Magic show to see the orders, so I held back on purchases. We did work with Antonio before the show and, once again, Laurie and I took a cautious approach to product development. We followed the same plan with Scott Chin and our friends in Italy. Because of the unknown, it was tough trying to stay positive. We had no idea how to prepare from month to month. We could be in business for a few months or might be doing the same thing next year if there was no sale. It was maddening.

In early February, I read in the industry trade journal about a ladies' shoe company in California, Sunwest Footwear. They purchased a belt company located across the street from our warehouse in Phoenix.

I called someone I knew at the company to request an introduction to the firm's principals. In less than twenty-four hours, I received a call from the vice president of marketing, Bob Perry, and we discussed their interest in our company. He invited Mike and me to visit their office in California to meet the owner of the firm, and we set a date for February 24.

We coincided the date with the end of the shoe show in Las Vegas and flew to John Wayne airport in Orange County, rented a car and drove to their office.

We met Jim Lindell and Bob and showed them the virtual video of the company. They were well-prepared and had checked out the company with many of our accounts and people who knew me personally, including Dick Braeger from Gary's.

There was no negotiating the price. I made that clear from the start of the meeting. They agreed to receive copies of our financial statements for the past three years and signed a nondisclosure statement. Mike showed them our financials on his computer.

Jim promised us he would get back to us within a week, and Mike and I returned to the airport. He flew to Phoenix and I to Chicago. Before proceeding to our respectful gates, Mike asked my opinion, and I told him, "They will buy the company. It is a perfect match for them."

Laurie and I continued to prepare for the coming trip to Italy. Once again, we decided to forgo Spain.

In early March, we flew to Rome, intending to spend just the day of arrival, and checked into Hotel Art, a new hotel I had read about. It was on a great street, Via Margutta, which once had been a bustling commercial district. It had started a significant comeback with galleries, clothing stores, restaurants, and hotels.

The hotel originally was a sixteenth-century monastery, and the lobby ceiling was restored as it was in the late 1500s. We were escorted to our room and were pleased. We found a new home in Rome. The best part was it was half the price of the Inghilterra.

We were tired from being on the plane for ten hours where neither of us slept well, so we decided to forgo any shopping. We rested for a while, and then we walked to a new pizza restaurant in the area called Fiore Fiore. It far surpassed the place near the Pantheon.

After, we walked to Caffe Greco for an espresso to help us stay awake, and we ended up sitting on the Spanish Steps. The hot sun was good; it was still cold in Chicago when we left.

I closed my eyes to try to relax. My mind was in a constant state of flux, going back and forth regarding the future. The fate of Paradise Shoe Company and what to do about Sensi if the company sold.

We left for Firenze the next morning and arrived early afternoon and went for focaccia and our fix. We walked with no plan to window shop. We had lost the momentum, the desire, the drive. It was an empty, sad feeling.

That night, we went to a new ristorante around the corner from via Tornabuoni called Buca Lapi and had excellent cuisine. I use that word to describe the meal because this was a find! It was so good we made a reservation to return the next night. We had fresh homemade pasta served with sautéed mushrooms in a very light reduced vegetable broth sauce. We shared a veal Milanese chop that had been lightly breaded, and Laurie reminded me to make sure the restaurant went into my book for future visits.

Our next two days to Vanni and Valore remain a blur. My mind was not there. I depended on Laurie to carry the ball, which she did. I was not sleeping well. My mind was preoccupied with the unknowns. My brain felt like a billiard ball, bouncing from one cushion to the other. Paradise Shoes one moment, Sensi the next, interest rates, then the factories and our employees entered. They will be looking for a job once the company sells. Where does that leave Antonio? Juan Jose had already started construction on his addition to the belt factory. Scott Chin had three kids in college, one in the States!

Georgio at Rosetta had built a new home in the hills of Verona, and Lidia and the group at the factory were counting on us. We were, by far, their number one customer.

At breakfast, I shared my thoughts with Laurie, and she tried to comfort me. "Joe, you have to remember we did well by all those people for the past six years. Maybe whoever buys the company will continue to do business with them. You are a good salesman. Sell them on the idea of keeping the ball rolling. Don't fix what is working. Our track record speaks for itself. Why would anyone want to screw it up?"

"Laurie, do you remember what happened when Deckers bought Sensi? It took them less than two years to destroy what took us years to build!"

I fell asleep on the train to Milano. Michael Tolaini was waiting for us, and we went to the factory and worked. We took a late afternoon train to Verona.

We gave Lidia a monster hug. She always brightened the cloudiest day; she was always up. We went for pizza and then to the Hotel Victoria, and I fell asleep the minute my head hit the pillow.

The next morning, I called Mike from a private office at Rosetta.

"Dad, I have some good news. Sunwest Footwear sent two accountants here, and they are verifying the inventory report off the computer, checking the arrival data of products in the warehouse to assure that it is all current!"

"How long have they been there?"

"They are almost finished."

"This is serious, Mike. Sounds good." I could not help but think how watching the inventory closely was paying off.

"How are you guys doing? Dad, have you told the factories anything?"

"Only Lidia knows, and it is keeping me up nights."

"I know. I have the same problem. I am concerned about all the help here and the salespeople. They have put their hearts and soul into this. I dread telling them. I had to tell a lie about the two auditors. I told them they were from the factor. I hate myself for that."

"Mike, don't beat yourself up about it. This goes on all the time. Every time a business is sold, people are displaced. Sometimes it works out for the best. I am going to do everything I can to sell whoever buys it, to leave well enough alone. Let's take it one day at a time."

On top of all this, I had another concern. Two of our sales guys had developed lung cancer, Paul Evans in San Francisco and my good friend Larry Brenner in Dallas. I had known Larry since the sixties. I attended his wedding to Michelle, and the sad note was both those guys were in excellent health when they were diagnosed. Neither had ever smoked. Paul had three kids. Michelle and Larry had a son. All I could think of was what would happen to their families.

When I finished my conversation with Mike, I just sat alone in that office. The thought of going back to the table to look at shoes was the last thing in the world I wanted to do. I could not wait to get on the train and go home.

I finally realized I was not being fair to Laurie, nor Rudy and Lidia who had worked diligently putting the collection together, and I needed to show them some respect. I returned to the sample room and we finished the new line.

That night, I suggested to Lidia and Rudy we go to the old olive oil ristorante, Al Beati, and have a nice dinner. It was our treat, and I ordered a bottle of Amarone. For two hours, I focused on sharing a great dinner and our new favorite red wine. Lidia knew where my head was. She was that perceptive. She did not have to say it. I could sense it when she dropped us off at the hotel. She got out of the car and gave me a bear hug, and I noticed a tear in her eye, and it took all I could muster to keep from crying myself. There was one definite thing. If we leave the shoe business, the relationship with Lidia will remain the rest of our lives!

We took the train to Rome and arrived early afternoon, checked into the Hotel Art, went for pizza, and afterward walked down to Via del Corso. The streets were crowded, so we turned up the via Condotti and strolled back to the room and took a nap before dinner. We were both exhausted. We had reservations at Hosteria del Pesce and promised each other to enjoy the evening and not discuss the circumstances. We took a taxi to Campo dei Fiore. It was crowded, so the driver dropped us off at the entrance, and we walked through the crowd. It never ceases to amaze me how vibrant that piazza is.

Home again, where Chicago was experiencing the last days of winter, it took me a few days to get back into the regular routine.

Laurie continued pursuing the 2006 spring line, and I cautiously reordered basics. I was buying with a mindset as if we were going out of business.

In June, we finally received an official offer from Sunwest Footwear. It was for the full asking price, with only one challenge. They wanted a ten percent holdback for one year, pending revenue on my sales projections for the period from August 2005 to July 31, 2006. I had purposely severely reduced the projections assuming they would try that. We agreed, and the sale agreement went to the attorneys with a closing date of August 7.

The week before the closing, Mike received a call from Tony Margolis, stating that the president of the retail stores wanted to return $1.3M worth of shoes. At their cost, that came to $585,000. Mike called me with the news, and it blew the top of my head off! I called Margolis in a rage. "Tony, this will blow our deal! You can't let this happen!"

Tony was sympathetic, but he said, "Joe, I know you are upset. Come up with a way to resolve it, and I will approve it, but the goods have to leave our warehouse in the next week. We are overstocked, and the warehouse has to clean out to accept fall merchandise coming in."

I called Mike and gave him the news about the discussion with Tony. "Here is what we are going to do. Find a place to receive the shoes. It can't go into our warehouse. Sunwest had agreed to use it and our people until they could get things set up in a public warehouse somewhere in the Midwest. Get me an inventory of what they want to return by style and color. I will go to work and get it sold at our cost, and once we get the number, whatever it is, I will ask Tony to approve it, and then we credit the stores. None of this has to be part of the transaction with Sunwest."

Mike called his friend at UPS, and they accepted the shipment, and in less than forty-eight hours, I sold the shoes to a national outlet chain that carried the best brands. They promised they would not advertise the name. Problem solved. I couldn't help but think back to my old Italian/Sicilian neighborhood in St. Louis, where that company store president would have received a visit from a couple of guys, and they would not be there to take him to lunch.

Sunwest signed the agreement on the seventh. It should have been a happy day, but it was a sad day for all of us. Three days before the deal closed, Larry Brenner and Paul Evans lost their battles with cancer. I am not ashamed to say I shed a few tears. It minimized my problems, and I did some self-criticism. It took every bit of mental capacity I could muster to call Michelle Brenner and Paul's wife to offer my condolences.

As part of the deal with Sunwest, Laurie and I signed an agreement to continue product development for a year, which included the teams in Spain, Italy, and China. Mike also signed a contract to stay on as national sales manager. His deal was for two years.

We did not attend the Magic show. Sunwest had its own booth. A few of our reps were there, but very few orders were taken. Mike was doing his job and working with reps across the country. Laurie continued working on the fall 2006 lines, doing her job with as much vigor as she could muster, but she admitted she did not have the same passion she once had.

I don't remember having a more stressful year, and I was elated when the ball dropped in Times Square on New Year's Eve, ending 2005. I thought about a recent dinner with our photographer friend, Dave Phillips and his wife Sue, where the conversation drifted to Italy. Laurie and I spent time discussing our favorite cities, the restaurants, the sights, and we sprinkled our conversation with history. By the end of the evening, we decided to take a trip with them in 2006.

CHAPTER 17

Pleasure with the Phillips 2006

I n January, Sunwest hired a new staff to run the Tommy Bahama division purchased from us. On February first, Laurie and I were dismissed. They paid us through August. They also fired Antonio, as well as the rest of our international team. My worst nightmare became reality! We were devastated.

I exploded. "This is textbook on how to screw up a great business. I give them two years, and they will lose the license because the quality of the product will decline, and sales will drop substantially. They will cut commission rates on the salespeople, and this, coupled with taking production to China and other parts of Asia, will destroy what it took us seven years to build. They will benefit from this season; the momentum is there because we did this season's line. It's their company, and it will no longer be a family-oriented team. I feel for our people at the factories."

"I agree, Joe. They had a great opportunity to transition, using Antonio and me until they get to meet the people at the factories that took us to the dance. They are idiots."

In June, they fired Mike Reina but had to honor his contract for the balance of eighteen months.

At lunch with Dave Phillips, I discussed our planned trip to Italy. We met Dave and Sue in 2000, and I learned that he was from my hometown St. Louis, and we went to rival high schools. He is one of the world's great semi-retired photographers.

Dave was pleased with the May itinerary. "Joe, we are in your hands. We have never been to Italy and are very excited. Just let me know what you need from us in the way of money."

In May, we flew to Milano from Rome and stayed at the Gallia, where both rooms were upgraded. I suggested Sue and Dave take a shower and get refreshed, and meet us in the lobby in an hour. We took a taxi to Via Monte Napoleone and walked the streets, enjoying a warm sunny blue sky day. We had a noon reservation to see *The Last Supper* and arrived early to find reservations for them recorded, but none for Laurie and me. My poor Italian did not work in the attempt to convince the reception person to allow us to go in. Soon, Sue and Dave were escorted in by a young man with a group of nineteen others. We were seated just outside the door leading into that room. When the young man returned, Laurie complimented him on his sneakers. Looking at her, he said, *"No capisco."* (I don't understand.) I translated in my poor Italian, *"Signora piace le tua scarpe."* (The lady likes your shoes.)

He said, *"Sei Siciliano?"* (You are Sicilian?) I replied again in Italian, "I am American, but my parents were born in Casteltermini."

He lit up like a Christmas tree and replied that he was born in Casteltermini and asked our name. When I told him, again he was shocked. His cousin had married a Reina from the town! We agreed it had to be a relative. We were the only Reinas in the village. When the next group convened, he let us enter with them. Once again, Laurie's inquisitive mind worked on our behalf. We were astounded to see that the artist restoring *The Last Supper* had made incredible progress. The darkness that once covered it had disappeared.

We rendezvoused with Sue and Dave and took a taxi to the Duomo di Milano. Always, no matter how many times we visited it, we could only marvel at the magnificent cathedral. I explained the history to them, and after photos by Dave, we entered.

We crossed the street and showed them the Galleria, and after walking around, we stopped for an espresso. Again, I explained the history. It was a joy to share the facts, and Sue commented, "Your knowledge about everything so far has made this trip extraordinary. I am more excited now than when we left home." We walked back to Via Monte Napoleone and had lunch in the garden at Il Salumaio. I could see they were tiring, so afterward, we headed back to the hotel and rested before dinner. That night, we had dinner at Antica Trattoria Della Pesa, and Sue joined Laurie for pasta alle Erbe, and Dave and I had Risotto Milanese. We shared the Apple Tarte Tatin.

We took the train to Verona the next morning and checked into the Hotel Victoria. Lidia and Stefano came to pick us up, and after showing Sue and Dave the sights, we strolled the shopping area on the way to Piazza delle Erbe for lunch. We took a walk afterward and showed more of the town, and returned to the hotel to change for dinner. Lidia had made dinner reservations at the old olive oil factory, and we ordered for the table, prosciutto con melon, great pasta, and roasted vegetables, and a bottle of Amarone. Neither Sue nor Dave had ever had it. Dave was very impressed. We ate by candlelight. It was a clear moonlit night and the stars lit up the cloudless sky.

The next day, Lidia took us to Sirmione on the lake. The weather was outstanding, sunny, and warm. We had lunch at a very nice *osteria* and later gelato, another first for Sue and Dave.

That night, we drove up to Belvedere for tortellini. Dave said, "If I lived here and ate like this, I would weigh 300 pounds." I said, "No, Dave. We are walking so much that would never happen. Have you noticed there are hardly any obese Italians?" We gave Lidia a big hug when she took us back to the hotel, and I noticed a tear in her eye when her hug moved around to Laurie. I knew what she was thinking. We no longer would be doing business with her. "Will I ever see the two of you again?"

On Wednesday, we took the train to Firenze, and we checked into another Ferragamo hotel, The Continentale, and after unpacking, we took our companions for focaccia and shared a slice of pear tart for dessert.

We walked down to the Duomo, and again Dave took great photos. I gave them a brief history and told them we had a four o'clock reservation to meet a guide to visit the Uffizi Gallery, and that finished the day's sightseeing.

We took them to Buca Lapi for dinner and enjoyed another fabulous meal, family-style, pasta con piselli fresca (pasta with fresh spring peas).

After breakfast the next day, we went to see *Michelangelo's David*, and they were both shocked at the size. I purposely did not tell them about it. Dave took a large group of photos, and Sue once again stated how pleased she was. "There is no way we could have experienced what we have already seen if it were not for the two of you!"

Later, we walked to Piazza della Signoria for coffee and then to Michelangelo's home.

Dave was in a state of awe. He could not get over the fact that everything was in place 350 hundred years after the man's death.

We concluded the day with a visit to the Uffizi Palazzo and Palazzo Pitti.

That night, we dined at Taverna Branzino, another historic building. I explained when we were seated that it was the home of artist Agnolo di Cosimo (Branzino his artist name).

Dave asked, "How did you find this place?"

"Laurie heard about it through a friend years ago, and I put it in my book, and we have been eating here for years."

On Friday, we departed for our hideaway, Forte dei Marmi, and arrived in time for pizza at al Bocconcino, and after, we walked with no agenda. I explained this is usually where we do nothing but relax at the end of the trip. I could see they were both ready to just lie around the pool. For the next three nights, we had dinner at Maito, Tre Stelle, and climaxed the last night at Osteria del Mare.

On Monday, we boarded the train to Rome for the final two days of the trip. When we arrived, we took our favorite tour of the Trevi Fountain, Pantheon, and Piazza Navona. They got the history lesson and a slice of pizza as a bonus.

That night, we took them to Assunta Madre, a new fresh fish ristorante near Campo de Fiore.

After breakfast the following day, we went to the Colosseum, and Dave shot some unusual photos and finished the day at the Vatican. Again, they got the history of both. For our final dinner of the trip, we walked to Babette down the street from the Hotel Art.

When we got to the airport in Chicago, we said our goodbyes, having shared our experiences, in turn creating some fond memories for two of our best friends. Later we received a case of Amarone from Dave and Sue, which only enhanced our memories of the trip.

We did not return to Italy in 2007 or 2008. In 2009, we took the same trip with our friends Carol Fitzmaurice and Bill Jage. They also shared their gratitude for the time and effort we put into organizing the trip. I told them, "We enjoyed it too and even though we have visited the sights and eaten the food many times, we never tire of it."

One of the highlights was taking them to Venice for the day and having lunch at Harry's American Bar. We each had three Bellinis, which now had reached the price equivalent to twenty-four dollars. Our bar bill exceeded the food bill. Bill and I had been victims of the twenty percent prime rate debacle in the early eighties that ultimately put us out of business. We shared the lunch bill, and laughed at it. I said, "If someone had told me in 1981 I would be spending this kind of money for lunch, I would have told them they were out of their mind."

I am not sure if growing up without the dream of travel and financial success makes it any more rewarding but, I can assure you, it has for me. I treasure the people we met along the way, and the icing on the cake was traveling and sharing our love for Italy with friends, our coworkers from our company, and family members.

Colosseum interior, Rome, compliments of Dave Phillips

Forte dei Marmi, Italy

The author and Dave Phillips enjoying gelato

Joe and Laurie Reina eating pizza in Florence

Laurie and Joe Reina at the Galleria in Milan,
compliments of Dave Phillips

Sue Phillips and Laurie inside Cantinetta Verrazzano in Florence

The Statue of David in Florence, compliments of Dave Phillips

Uffizi Gallery in Florence, compliments of Dave Phillips

Santa Maria del Fiore Cathedral in Florence,
compliments of Dave Phillips

CHAPTER 18

Puglia 2018

In the ensuing years, Laurie and I traveled to Italy a few times with other family and friends, never tiring of introducing my amazing homeland. But we were not finished with our exploration. We had one area of Italy left on our bucket list. It was the southeast area, Puglia.

We wanted to reward Lidia for fifteen years of chauffeuring our friends and us all over the Verona area. We contacted Lidia to see if she and Stefano could join us in August. It was a "yes" for her, and Stefano agreed to be with us for a few days.

We shared the entire trip with her on the phone, six days in Puglia, a weekend in Verona, then a drive up to the Alps. Next by auto to Alba, and then the last weekend in Forte dei Marmi. Reluctantly, she agreed to be our guest. She wanted to pay her share, but I assured her that was not happening.

She met us at the airport in Rome, and together we flew to Brindisi for two nights. We had a hassle at the auto rental office, where she had made reservations with an Italian car rental agency. They had no record and no cars! We moved to Hertz, where I had a Number One card, and we got a car. We checked into our hotel Palazzo Virgilio Gesti for two nights. We were starving and walked by the sea and had a pizza. That night, we had dinner at Trattoria Pantagruele and had fresh grilled fish and roasted vegetables. The next day, we drove to a nearby town I had read about called Carovigno, a beautiful town a short ride from Brindisi, and we found a Michelin Star restaurant and made reservations for dinner that night. It was called Il Buongiorno. The meal was well worth the thirty-minute drive back. We shared a lobster filled ravioli to start and an incredible fillet of sea bass for our main course.

The next day, we drove to Ostuni, a mountain town. It dates back to Roman times. For dinner at Osteria Del Tempo Perso, we ordered the specialty, Parmigiana (baked thinly sliced eggplant layered with Parmigiano cheese). The unique thing we learned was Puglia reminded me of my first trip in 1980. There were hardly any tourists. The restaurants were not overcrowded, the prices for everything were moderate, the people seemed happier, and there was less stress.

We departed for Leece the next day. A friend had said it was like Firenze in 1940, and he was right. A hidden secret in the middle of nowhere. Beautiful sculptures and frescos all over the city, and after scouring the menus of many restaurants, we finally found Gemma, a small *osteria,* and settled for a very nice dish of pasta with marinara.

We continued to the town of Maglie and checked into our hotel, Corte del France Maglie. It had been a shoe factory at the turn of the last century, and there were displays of tools that were used when there were no machines to make shoes. They were handsewn!

Stefano joined us, and for the next three days, we drove to the southern part of Puglia, which included Gallipoli, Taranto, and a beautiful drive along the sea.

We headed north to Alberobello and checked into the Hotel La Corte dell'Astore, a quaint twelve-room gem run by a husband-wife team. The beautifully renovated building had been a small villa formerly owned by the husband's uncle. All the rooms were mini suites featuring aquariums and furnished lavishly. Dinner was at a local pizzeria that night.

The owner of the hotel had an American eagle, and after breakfast, took us to a hillside open area where he released the well-trained eagle to soar over the valley. With a signal of some kind from him, the eagle returned and landed on a thick leather sleeve he wore on his right arm. It was an incredible sight!

After feeding the eagle chicken pieces, he allowed Laurie to wear the leather sleeve and hold the eagle for a photo "op."

The next day, we drove to the ancient city of Matera that dates back 250 BC. It had been raped over the years by the Franks, Romans, and various Muslim groups.

People originally lived in caves that had been carved into the mountainsides and were still living in them as late as 1952. They were living literally like animals and had to be evacuated. The caves were cleansed of many diseases and then carefully restored, using existing furnishings that had survived hundreds of years. After touring the caves, we ate lunch in town and returned to Alberobello. That night, we dined at Favola in Tavola Ristorante in Alberobello.

Stefano departed for Rome the next morning, and we flew from Brindisi to Verona for the weekend and stayed at Hotel Academia. We had the best pizza in all of Italy that night at Pizzeria Teodorico. The dough was soft and moist and had a fresh flavor, almost like cake. We had never had any pizza as good anywhere in Italy or the United States.

On Sunday, we went to the lake with Lidia, and Stefano returned to join us for lunch in Sirmione at Ristorante Risorgimento. It was the first time we had eaten there, and it was not to be the last. It went into my book. That night, I insisted we have tortellini, and they took us to La Borsa.

On Monday, we headed north to the Alps and checked into a beautiful hotel called Baeren Hotel Zum in Valdora.

It was all-inclusive, very Austrian, and we had dinner family style.

The next morning, Lidia and Laurie took a gondola up to the top of the mountain and shot some great photos.

We drove to Alba the next day and arrived in time for dinner and checked into the Hotel Callissano Alba and were shocked at the newly remodeled rooms. We dined at Osteria Dell'Arco, and another surprise, the food was incredible. We had pasta with truffles.

Alba is an ancient city, famous for the truffle auctions in the fall, where it is said that the best white truffles in Italy are found in the hills and mountains around the city.

This was originally to be a stopping point for the final part of the trip, which was Forte dei Marmi. But we found it to be fascinating.

Lidia projected the drive to Forte to be five hours. I tried to sleep, but my mind was drifting back to our arrival and how quickly the trip had gone. I knew Lidia would be departing for the long drive back to Verona after dropping us off. I tried to convince her to stay one night, but she declined.

I wondered when we would see her and Stefano again. The same thought surfaced about any return to Italy. Laurie fell asleep in the front seat, so there was no dialogue between the girls. My mind continued to drift and finally settled on 2017 and the two trips we had taken the previous year.

In May, we took my son, Mike, his wife, Susan, and my grandsons, Evan and Brock. We spent three days in Rome, four in Firenze, and one in Lucca. We had a guide in Rome and shared our favorite sites and restaurants. Evan, who was in fifth grade, had studied the history of Rome in third grade, and his choices of places to see were contrived from his notes in third grade. I recalled what I was thinking in third grade. It was far from Rome—real far! No words to describe how far. There are no words to describe my childhood compared with Evan's. I was a Depression kid, first-generation, brainwashed to understand there was no money for extravagant things. There was not the slightest thought of ever traveling to Italy, even as a young adult.

My mind returned to Lidia. We shared fifteen years of sites, scenes, stories, and our love for the best country in the world.

We reached Forte dei Marmi late afternoon and ate pizza with Lidia at Bocconcino, and finished at our favorite gelato shop. We knew it was that time.

We hugged, and all three of us shed a few tears. We promised never to forget our friendship. I said, "Lidia, you have our word. We will never return without seeing you! We love you."

It was an emotional ending to one of our best trips ever. Laurie was more upset and emotional than I was. At dinner that night, I calmed her down and promised the next time we returned, we would go in August. I said I would arrange for two rooms at our hotel in Forte and have her stay with us, and we will tour Tuscany!

And so it ends for now. Half of my life has passed since that first trip in 1980. There are people in this world who have possibly traveled more, spent more money, traveled more lavishly, eaten in fancier restaurants, and stayed in more expensive hotels, but I know no one on this earth who has had a better time, met more interesting people, or enjoyed themselves more.

Lidia and Stefano Turati in Alberobello with eagle

Lidia, Stefano at our trulia in Alberobello, Puglia

Matera, Italy

Ostuni, Puglia

Trulia houses in Alberobello

EPILOGUE

I once was asked if I had to live my life all over again, what would I change? I took not a moment to respond. "I waited until I was forty-four years old before going to Italy!"

At a very young age, my older brother, Jim, started pounding in my head. "Life goes by quickly. We are only on this earth a damn hot minute. Grab it with both hands, Joe, and enjoy every minute."

That's all well and good, but he did not explain all the stumbling blocks along the way. I call them excuses. I got married young and had two children quickly and a third unexpectedly three years later. We had house payments and car payments, and going abroad was cost-prohibitive. Italy was not on my radar.

Then, a divorce pushed the thought of traveling to Italy way down the list of any dreams. In fact, there were a series of nightmares sandwiched between some actual successful years before reaching my forty-fourth year.

Sometimes in life, the page turns in the great book up there, and people and various things converge to influence our lives. There are many examples of this that leaped into mine. Friends who traveled to Italy were constantly shoving it into my face. "Joe, when are you going to visit your homeland? You have no idea what you are missing."

That first trip provided the injection of desire to return. Italy got under my skin.

The books I read played their part. The most influential was Robert Hughes' *Rome*. I read two other books on Italy that played to the desire to go back. Then I read the 3000-year history of Sicily. It also sparked the need to visit, to say nothing of the fact that my parents were born there.

I would be remiss if I failed to mention Sensi and that family, their trust, and confidence.

The relationships of the people at all the factories had a significant impact on us. Then there's the sadness of no longer breaking bread with them. My concern for them losing our business has preyed on my mind for the last fifteen years. Sadly, the Rosetta factory hit on hard times and had to shut down.

And then there is Lidia and Stefano. That relationship is a bright spot and shall remain so for the rest of our lives.

I have sent so many people on trips, specifically designed to their wishes and personalities, and enjoyed sharing our experiences with them. Everyone has said, "Joe, you need to write a book about Italy."

I finally agreed to combine the fun and excitement of the years, with the idea in mind to be of some service to the reader to ensure a good time, along with a cultural, historical, and learning experience. Through this book are names of hotels, sites, and restaurants to also experience. My hope is to make sure younger people avoid the mistake I made of waiting too long.

It is my desire that this book inspires those that have never been to go and to those that have been to return.

Behind the frescos, the great sites, fountains like Trevi, beautiful piazzas, churches, statues, paintings—the arts that created the Renaissance—lie the fascinating stories of the fabulous but flawed artists whose brilliance was driven by the creative urge as it was by their egos' need to out—do and belittle the artistic works of their rivals in a creative atmosphere funded by and controlled by the wealthy patrons whom the artists had to win favor with to get commissions to fund their careers. Thus, Italy's poets, artists, architects, and creative geniuses and competitive juices flowed as they strove to one—up all artistic comers and their gifts and aesthetic talents enabled first Rome and later Italy, to become the mecca of artistic achievement that draws a global audience to visit her timeless treasures each year!

My extensive conversations with residents of Italy's landmark sites have provided insights into places inherently of interest, but little known insights this book offers on what's worth seeing and learning about that the "standard tour" can't provide: the root stories of historical events and sites that make them come alive.

Marsala, Sicily

Piazza del Duomo Siracusa, Sicily

ABOUT THE AUTHOR

Joe Reina was born of Sicilian immigrants in St. Louis, Missouri, on February 7, 1936. He attended Shaw Grade School and graduated from Southwest High School. He began working at the Arrow Shirt company in September 1954 while taking night classes at St. Louis University. Later, as a salesman for Arrow, he was promoted to district manager in the firm's Chicago office in 1970. He continued his education for three years, taking night classes at Northwestern University.

Early, while in Chicago to hedge against excessive income tax, Joe ventured into real estate. Throughout his adult life, most of his business career kept him involved in the apparel industry. It required international travel and enabled him to explore a good part of the world. This book is based on his meticulous notes while traveling more than forty times to Italy. Such travel helped satisfy his desire to share those experiences with his family and friends and relive the pleasure of those special moments.

Joe is retired and lives in Scottsdale, Arizona.

CPSIA information can be obtained
at www.ICGtesting.com
Printed in the USA
JSHW061950250722
28494JS00001B/4